D.W. Talbot   1988.

THE BEST OF
DICK
WALKER'S
COARSE FISHING

THE BEST OF
DICK WALKER'S
COARSE FISHING

Edited by
PETER MASKELL

DAVID & CHARLES
Newton Abbot   London   North Pomfret (Vt)

(page 2) *A 4lb perch – a fish most anglers can only dream about. This fish was taken by the author from Arlesey Lake, the water that gave its name to one of his many inventions, the Arlesey bomb.*

British Library Cataloguing in Publication Data

Walker, Richard, 1918–1985
 The best of Dick Walker's coarse fishing.
 1. Fishing
 I. Title II. Maskell, Peter
 799.1'1   SR 439

 ISBN 0-7153-9089-9

Typeset by ABM Typographics Limited, Hull
and printed in Great Britain
by Redwood Burn Ltd, Trowbridge, Wilts
for David & Charles Publishers plc
Brunel House   Newton Abbot   Devon

Published in the United States of America
by David & Charles Inc
North Pomfret   Vermont 05053   USA

PREFACE

Countless words have been written about fishing for many hundreds of years, but Dick Walker must have been the most prolific writer of all time.

Articles published in various angling papers are not easily accessible in later years and, as so many readers have told us of their deep enjoyment in reading and re-reading Richard's books, Peter Maskell has kindly once again used his special skills in collating another selection of articles. This time the material was previously published in *Angling Times.*

Where possible we have given the names of the photographers but we apologise to other friends if we have used their photographs without proper acknowledgment.

PAT MARSTON WALKER

To all Richard's readers and fishing friends, including those he held in especial affection, whose companionship along the way enriched his writings, but in particular is remembered Peter Thomas, the most loyal and unswerving of friends since childhood.

Pat Marston Walker

CONTENTS

INTRODUCTION

Dick Walker was the greatest angling writer of all time. For thirty years he contributed a weekly column to the world's best-selling angling newspaper, *Angling Times*. The Dick Walker column rapidly established itself as one of the most important and widely-read pages in the newspaper.

Yet it was the quality, not the quantity of Dick's writing that made him so revered. He refused to write about any part of the sport of which he had no practical experience... but during that thirty years wrote authoritatively about every conceivable method and tactic!

All his writings were based on practical fishing experience and exhaustive experimentation. His list of fish catches is endless, from record carp to record trout. His sheer genius for problem solving is preserved for ever in the form of such examples as the Arlesey bomb, beta-light floats and countless standard trout fly patterns; and the Grinner knot named after his son Robert's early nickname.

His untimely death in 1985 robbed us of an angling genius; our only consolation the sheer volume of knowledge that survives with his written work.

This book contains just a sample of that genius, fifty articles selected from more than a thousand. I think Dick would have approved of the choice – and if he hadn't he would have told me so in no uncertain terms before offering me a consolation drink!

Read the book, enjoy it and, above all, have fun when you're fishing.

That's the way Dick would have wanted it.

Peter Maskell 1988

PART I
GENERAL

There are much bigger fish to catch

I've just been discussing with a friend the matter of which kind of fish is most likely to produce the next record-breaker. I voted for the tench, but the whole discussion made me recall the big fish of various kinds that I have seen, or heard about, from anglers whose honesty and ability to judge well the size of fish in the water are beyond question.

I have never actually set out to break records, because I don't consider them very important. The chap who has caught the biggest fish ever of any species is not necessarily the best angler, and that was never more clearly demonstrated than in 1952.

In June of that year, Pete Thomas and I were carp-fishing, with our baits only a few yards apart. Pete caught a carp of 28lb 10oz, a much bigger fish than I had ever caught at that time.

In September of the same year, our baits again lay within a few yards of one another. Mine was taken by a 44-pounder. Now, only a fool would think that Pete was a better carp-fisher than I only between June and September in 1952! Actually, he's better than I am any time!

No, the mark of a good angler for any kind of fish is that he can catch consistently fish above the average weight for their species, in the various differing waters in which they are found.

Because this is the aim of chaps like Bernard Venables, Pete Thomas, Maurice Ingham and several more I could mention. Because we have found that it pays to spend a lot of time searching for the fish, and in general observation, before we start the actual fishing, most of us have, at one time or another, seen some fish a lot bigger than we have ever succeeded in landing.

I would go so far as to say that there are few species of fish of which there are not much bigger examples swimming about than have ever been landed.

Of the various species, the kind of which I have seen most potential record-breakers is the tench. I've seen tench upwards of 10lb in weight in at least four different waters and I think some of them were 12lb or more. In fact, I have seen as many as a dozen all together, any one of which would beat the present record very easily.

On top of that, lots of friends who are keen on tench tell me that they have seen quite a lot of fish of similar calibre, which is why I think a new record for tench is likely before very long.

I've seen quite a lot of big chub upwards of 6lb, and caught one or two; but only twice have I seen chub that I was sure would top the record of 8½lb. One was so very dead that I couldn't weigh it. It lay in a cow-drink and measured 27 inches.

I hope
The other was, and I hope is, alive, and I hope also, one day to be able to tell you exactly what it weighs.

Everyone has heard of Arlesey perch, and there I have seen fish that I am sure are over 6lb and may easily top 7lb. But I am told, and I believe it, that double-figure perch exist.

There are without doubt record-breaking barbel, certainly in the Hampshire Avon, where Roy Beddington actually caught one over 16lb while spinning for salmon, but unfortunately it was in the close season and didn't count.

The former British record tench, a fish of 12lb 11½oz. This magnificent specimen was taken by Andrew Wilson from Wilstone Reservoir, Tring. The current record stands at 14lb 5oz (Angling Times)

Otters have also produced certain evidence of barbel bigger than have ever been caught by anglers, and 20lb isn't by any means impossible.

I think there are record-breaking barbel in the Kennet and the Thames – that 14-pounder caught last back-end only needed to grow an ounce or two more.

Despite the jump taken in the carp-record, there are yet bigger carp swimming about. The carp is a fish that my friends and I always underestimate when we see them in the water. I can give you plenty of examples, but will content myself with two.

When I caught a carp for a broadcast in June last year, lots of anglers who listened heard me say, after I had got the fish under some sort of control, that it was about 12lb; the scales said 16½lb.

The big chap in the aquarium was practically an old friend when it was eventually landed; being easily distinguished from other carp in the water, nearly every member of the Carp Catchers' Club had seen it swimming about and had a guess as to its weight; and they all guessed somewhere between 30 and 35lb, except 'B.B.', who, as befitted the President, said between 35 and 40.

We have also seen, and some of us have hooked and lost, carp that we all guessed at well over 40lb, and in more than one water. Of them all, one that Pete Thomas and I spotted together stands out in my memory, for it made every other carp we have seen look no more than medium-sized.

When people ask us just how big we think carp can grow in Britain, we say 'Perhaps 60lb' – and then we remember that fantastic monster we saw, and look at one another, and wonder.

Only once have I seen a pike that I thought might top 40lb. It seized a 3½lb bream and not even a tail showed outside its mouth. But speculating on the weight of pike is such dangerous ground that I had better keep off it.

I've never seen a bream, or a rudd, or a dace, that looked to me like a record-breaker, but I don't doubt they exist, and nor does Mr E. G. Costin in the case of bream, for which he holds the record with a 13½-pounder.

As far as I can remember, no angler has ever broken his own record, but it wouldn't astonish me if Mr Costin became the first to do it.

Record roach

Once I saw a roach that looked every ounce of 4lb, and only once. More anglers fish for roach than for any other fish, so if there are many about over the 3lb 14oz record, it ought not to be long before one is caught.

As it is, very few roach within ½lb of the record are caught, and I am inclined to think that the roach record will stay as it is for a long time yet, unless a new water is discovered, or made, in which roach grow bigger than in any at present known. So now it is up to the MWB experts to prove me wrong!

As for gudgeon, plenty of anglers know that they could go and catch record gudgeon any day; probably, like me, they would be ashamed to make any claim if they did so.

I think the sooner the gudgeon, and all species that never reach even ½lb, are eliminated from specimen-fish competitions, the better. What could be more stupid than a 2oz gudgeon beating a 20lb carp?

About crucian carp and silver bream there is not much to be said. Such confusion has existed in the past, and enough exists now, about identification of these species that until anglers generally are better-informed it is safest to forget these fish.

Lastly, there's the eel. Now, there are without doubt eels in Britain whose size is terrific. The present record of something over 8lb is certainly less than half what is possible, and probably eels of 20lb and more exist.

I've seen some whackers myself, and been broken by some enough to know that landing one of the real monsters would need tackle far stouter than anyone who hooks one of these giants by accident is ever likely to be using.

The eel, in my opinion, isn't regarded as seriously as it deserves, but any angler who decides to specialise in fishing for big eels has an exciting career ahead of him.

No, not me! I'm just plain scared!

18 June 1954

A sixth sense in fishing

This week I'm going to run the risk of being thought crazy. I'm going to talk about something that may not be believed, isn't generally understood and is hard to explain.

Success in angling comes from many things and I have always said that much of it comes from logical, intelligent thinking. Skill of hand plays a part, sometimes a very important part, but sound thinking comes first, specially when you are after big fish.

I have to admit, though, that although an angler can succeed by using his brains and skill in combination, there is something else that can make him a good deal more successful; something that it is difficult to name. I have heard it called instinct.

Quite dark
For many years I knew that I could sometimes tell when a big fish, especially a big carp, was approaching my bait, even when it was quite dark and there was nothing to be seen or heard.

I have sat quietly, relaxed, and then suddenly become alert and ready, knowing that a bite would come in a minute or two. I never mentioned this to anyone, because I expected to be told I wasn't taking enough water with it.

Then one night in 1951, I was fishing with Maurice Ingham for carp in the dark. We were sitting only a yard or two apart, almost dozing, and suddenly I had that old feeling that a big fish was close to the bait. I sat up with a jerk and knelt by my rod, waiting – and then I heard a rustle on my right, and looking, saw in the gloom that Maurice, too, was crouched with his hand poised over the butt of his rod – and I realised that he had sensed the approach of a fish, too.

Best spot
This instinct shows up in another way, which I expect many anglers have noticed. In any swim or pitch, there is only one best spot. You can catch fish all over the swim, but at one spot you'll catch more than anywhere else, or perhaps bigger fish.

Now there's nothing queer about that, there are dozens of reasons why fish should prefer one definite spot in a swim. The current may suit them; they may like the bottom; there may be natural food attracting them, or even someone's groundbait.

Now, very often you can think out where that best spot is. You can size up the current, the wind, the weed, the depth, and work out in your mind the right spot, and find you were correct. Sometimes of course, you can actually see the fish; sometimes you find them by casting in different places, or by trotting down and noting the place where you get most bites.

But have you ever looked at a swim, and without any investigation or thinking, suddenly known where the best spot was; and known exactly where your bait would have to be cast to catch the fish you were after? Or, if you haven't, have you ever fished with another angler whose ability to pick the right place – the exact spot – seemed almost uncanny?

Now, I shouldn't have mentioned this if I hadn't got a theory about it, and if I didn't think it could be helpful to other anglers. I expect by now a good many readers are thinking that we're entering the realms of black magic, or something of that kind. We aren't! My theory about all this may sound far-fetched, but it doesn't involve anything irrational.

This is what I think the explanation is. I think we all possess remnants of senses and instincts that civilisation has shoved so far back into the background that we don't realise we have them.

In our ordinary lives we have no need of them. There was a time not so many thousands of years ago when these instincts were very useful indeed – essential perhaps, when man succeeded at hunting and fishing or else died of starvation. A few thousand years of not needing these instincts have nearly bred them out of us – but not quite.

Such people

There are races of men in the world today who live in a way which still demands these instincts, and those who have lived among such people will tell you that such instincts are possessed and used by them to a remarkable degree.

You will be asking – if you haven't dismissed the whole thing as preposterous – whether you have these instincts and if so, how you can make use of them. I can answer that, I think everyone has such instincts, deep down, to some degree.

This is how you can try to get yours working. Choose your swim by conscious thinking, as you always should. Fix up your tackle and get everything ready. Then before you start fishing, sit and study that swim for a few minutes. Don't try to think about it; just look at it. You may find that you are beginning to concentrate on a particular spot.

If you feel any such tendency, don't resist it. Let your mind relax. I shouldn't wonder if you find your concentration growing stronger; that one particular spot, one exact spot, is attracting you like a magnet, and that in some way which you can't explain to anyone, you suddenly know exactly where your bait must go.

You may not get results at first, but it's worth keeping on trying; and when you once have experienced this inner conviction about the right spot in a swim, you'll find you can get it more often and more strongly in the course of your fishing, wherever you may go.

I expect nine out of ten readers will dismiss all I've written on this subject with a hearty laugh; and no doubt I shall hear numerous wisecracks about it.

But not, I think, from the consistently successful experienced anglers. They will know very well that there are plenty of examples in their own experience, of the kind of thing I've tried to describe, although I doubt if they'll risk admitting it!

19 August 1955

So the fish can't spot violet – but it *can* see

I've come to the conclusion that more nonsense is talked about what fish can or cannot see than almost any other aspect of angling.

For example, in the last ten years or so i've read, or been told, that fish see everything in monochrome; that they can't see red; that they can't see violet, and, most certainly, in *Anglers Annual*, that they 'view the world as through orange glasses'.

It seems to be generally accepted, and it is said that experiments have proved, that fish see colours, but somewhat differently from humans. They cannot see colours at the violet end of the spectrum, but they can see more at the red end; into the infra-red region, in fact, which means that some blacks, or what to us are blacks, appear to fish as a colour that we cannot really imagine, but which has red as its basis – if that is a correct way of looking at it.

Curious conclusions

People who accept that this is so sometimes draw the most curious conclusions from it. Some years ago, it was argued that if fish are sensitive to violet light, then if we dyed our gut or nylon violet, the fish would be unable to see it. Violet-stained nylon was actually sold on that basis. People seriously believed that this would be invisible to fish.

Actually, of course, if fish cannot detect violet light, anything that is violet in colour will appear to them some shade of grey, or black, depending upon the intensity of the violet colour. A so-called colour is usually, in practice, a mixture of colours. A light or pastel colour is a mixture of all colours (white) plus one colour that predominates. A light violet line is reflecting more violet than any other colour. If a fish cannot see violet, such a line will appear to it grey. If a line could be dyed so that it reflected only violet light, then to a fish it would appear black.

So if you want your line to appear grey or black to fish, dye it grey or black! But be careful that black really is black and not infra-red!

Fallacious theory

This notion, that if fish are more sensitive to the red end of the spectrum, everything will appear to them as if seen through orange glasses, is of course entirely fallacious. The colours of the spectrum range from violet through indigo, blue, green, yellow and orange to red, as far as human vision can see.

If it proves the fact that fish cannot see violet and perhaps indigo, this does not mean they cannot see blue, green and yellow. They will see these colours just as we do. Looking through orange glasses reduces or removes all colours except orange, which is a very different matter from being unable to see particular colours.

So the fly-dresser, the maggot-dyer and the decorator of spinners can go ahead and use all the colours, in the sure knowledge that fish can see most if not all of them.

That is, of course, if fish really can't detect light from the blue end of the spectrum.

As I said, experiments are claimed to have shown that this is the case; but if it is true, it seems curious. Anyone who has dived deep in clear water knows that light from the blue end of the spectrum penetrates deepest, light from the red end least deep. Doesn't it seem odd that creatures evolved to live below the water, many of them well below, should be unable to detect the only light available to them below certain depths? Can we really believe that a land animal can still see in water at a depth where fish are blind?

Another fruitful source of misconception is what is called 'the trout's window'. I never could discover why it is so called, since the phenomenon applies to every kind of fish, but there it is, that's what it is called. It arises from the fact that rays of light passing from air to water or vice-versa within a certain angle are bent or, to use the scientific term, refracted, but at smaller angles to the surface, they are reflected. Because of this, it has been said that to a fish, the surface looks like a mirror with a circular hole in it, which is to some extent true, except that the hole has a beautiful rainbow all round its edge, and also, that the fish sees a very much wider area outside the hole than would be the case if it really were a hole in a mirror. It can see the angler easily enough, unless he takes care to prevent it. If you stand upright, a fish can see you, or part of you, if you're within about 20 yards; and 20 yards is about twice as far as most anglers think.

Another odd notion that has come up lately in respect of what fish can see is that because fish have no eyelids, and because their irises (the part around the pupil or lens of the eye, that the light passes through) can't expand and contract like that of a land animal, they must suffer from bright sunlight. I read somewhere that a fish suffers agonies when it is on the bank in sunshine, because of this. Somewhere else, I read that fish seek shade in bright sunshine because their eyes cannot accommodate.

Well, if that is so, how is it that provided they aren't scared, we often see them lying just below the surface on the hottest, brightest days of the year? Does the glare cause them agonies when they leap in the bright light, which they often do?

The fact is, fish have most remarkable eyes, that can function over a far wider range of light intensities than ours can. They can see well in much weaker light, and equally well in very bright light, as every experienced angler knows very well.

Vary the aperture

Physical movement of the iris to vary the aperture through which light passes is not the only way in which an eye can accommodate to varying light intensities.

It may be that fish can vary the sensitivity of their retinas, upon which the light passing through the lens of the eye falls. Be that as it may, fish can stand bright light all right, never doubt it.

The commonest misconception of all is that fish cannot see an angler when the water is muddy or rippled. That they cannot see him so clearly defined is true enough, but if any light reaches them at all, they can tell immediately if any object comes between them and its source, or part of its source. This means if you march up to the edge of the water with nothing behind you like a high bank, or a bush, then nearly all the fish within 20 yards will know you've arrived, whether the water be calm or rippled, clear, coloured or muddy.

If you fish on the assumption that in any light and in any conditions, fish can see a whole lot better than you can, you will catch many more than you will if you try to condone your own laziness and carelessness by arguing that their vision is defective.

30 December 1966

Night's the time when the senses come alive

I am sorry that so many anglers fail to understand what night fishing is all about. They think it is a means whereby big fish can easily be caught by somewhat doubtful methods. They don't want to try it themselves and in too many cases, they'd like to see it stopped so that nobody will have a better chance of catching a bigger fish than they do.

Nobody that I know fishes at night because he hopes that it will enable him to catch a bigger fish than his fellow anglers. It is possible, of course, that some have tried it for that reason, but they either give it up or, if they stay with it, it is because they have found a better reason. The better reason is enjoying being out fishing at night for its own sake.

I think most men have a subconscious desire to revert to a very primitive kind of life where deep-seated instincts and unrecognised abilities can be released. I think it is for such reasons that many men go in for fishing or wildfowling or birdwatching or other allied interests. They aren't out to compete with anyone. They want to prove to themselves that they can hold their own in a wild state.

Most of the time they don't understand what it is that makes them want to go out into the least civilised places they can find and shoot a goose or catch a fish. The urge is there nevertheless.

Most of us would like to fish a water that nobody has ever fished before, not because we think the fish would be easier to catch but because we visualise such places as being least affected by civilisation.

Another world
Fishing at night helps very much because then the daytime sights and sounds that constantly remind us that we live in a densely-populated small island are less obtrusive. At night you cannot see the row of pylons stretching across the countryside. Such noises as you do hear are usually far enough away to make you feel even more detached.

You may hear the rattle of a train or see the headlights of cars, but they are in a different world from yours. Yours is full of scents and sounds of the night.

The smell of hay and clover, of fir trees and bracken, of damp leaves and rushes, even of the water itself, are only really noticed by the night-fisher. The noise of a river is the same in daylight as in the dark, but you don't hear it in the daytime. At night that river is quicksilver, it chatters and babbles away, it sings, it croons, it whispers. On the lake, the water laps, the reeds rustle.

Sometimes on a clear night, you look up and are suddenly amazed at how many stars there are. Or there may be a river mist like cotton wool creeping up the stream towards you and then

Night fishing at Redmire. Pete Thomas grasps the landing-net mesh and another 20-pounder is safely landed

spilling out over the meadows, filling up all the hollows, and rising up in pillars like silent waterspouts. Then there comes a tiny breath of wind that makes the tops of the willows rustle, and in a few minutes all the mist has gone like magic.

Coots crying

There are times when the waterfowl decide to make a great ceremony of going to roost. Most nights they do it quite quietly, but now and then there are great flappings in the bushes and trees, and echoing cries of moorhens and coots, mixed with cracklings of twigs. You wonder what it is all about, but presently it settles down and you are suddenly aware of a deathly stillness.

Nothing moves, nothing makes a sound. It is as if you have suddenly become deaf. Then in this stillness you hear special, little noises. A mouse makes a tiny rustle in the grass. Suddenly comes a chorus of squeaks, then it stops and everything is quiet again.

You look up at the stars and there is a dark shape going across them with a 'wheesht wheesht wheesht' of wings. Wild duck? Moorhen? You will never know, but when you see a white, blurred shape move across the field, head high, against the dark trees, you know what that is, and you realise that you haven't heard the mice rustling for some time.

Far away a dog barks. It sounds very musical. Or is it a fox? From another direction comes an answer. It is a fox, you think. Have you ever seen how delicately a fox walks over dewy grass, or how he pounces like a cat if he spots a mouse out early? If you stay out fishing all night you will perhaps see that, and you may also see a badger or two, or even a deer coming down to drink, as it begins to lighten in the east.

Ripples die

Long before then, though, there will have been a considerable noise of wings as some mallards circle and land in the water, with a good deal of splashing, back, probably, from a raid on some farmer's wheat or barley field. They settle down with a little muted quacking, the ripples spread and die. A stronger breeze suddenly shakes the trees and you can hear dew falling. A little shiver goes down your back and you pull your coat more snugly round you.

Suddenly splash, whoomp! That was a real big one jumping.

The water fairly rocks. Slap-slap-slap come the waves against the bank. Wish that one would pick up the bait! It's been out there for five hours. Not a touch. Wonder if it's still on? Well – better leave it alone.

Flip-flip-flip – all the small fish are splashing about on the surface. It goes on for three minutes, then it stops as suddenly as it began. Why do they do it? Is it because this is the time when all the tiny things they eat come to the top? The daphnia, the cyclops and all those other teeming millions of tiny creatures. Well, you'll try and find out sometime. Very quiet now.

Chilly now
Gosh, it's chilly now. Get the flask out and have a cup of hot oxtail soup. A quiet voice 'You still awake?' 'Yes, anything doing?' 'I had a bit of a run an hour ago, but it stopped before I could strike. What about you?' 'Nothing yet!' 'That was a whopper that jumped a little while back – sounded like a cow falling in!' 'Yes, wish we could catch it! Here have some soup.' 'Thanks. Well, back to the rod.'

Quiet again – but the water is alive. It is lighter. The sky is turning from blue to purple and pink. Then tingallingaling – it's the bite alarm! The line is tearing out. Strike, and zeee-zeee-zeee goes the reel. 'Fish!'

Pad-pad of feet. 'Good one, is it? I've got the net!'

'It'll do!'

It'll do. It doesn't matter whether it is a bigger one than Bill caught last week. It doesn't matter what it is. It doesn't matter too much if it isn't even landed. It'll do. Because you've had your detachment from the office and the factory and the telly and the refrigerator and the smell of exhausts and the telephone and all those things. You've been a proper man for a while instead of a wretched puppet on strings that other people jerk.

Well, you go home, and while your're having your breakfast the postman pushes *Angling Times* through the letter box, and you unfold it, and there it is.

'Club official calls for Night-fishing Ban.'

27 January 1967

27

The rod as a painless aid to education

A few days ago, I was talking to a most intelligent non-angler about the unjust treatment anglers receive in the matter of grants from public bodies, in comparison with other sports.

When I mentioned the local Education Authority grants received by yachtsmen on the new reservoirs, he said: 'But you really can't call angling education, can you?'

He said it with a pitying sort of smile that left me in no doubt to what he was thinking – that there is no educational value in angling whatever.

It shocked me to realise that this is probably what most non-anglers think about fishing. It's the same old story; we anglers suffer from a public image that bears no relation to the truth.

The truth is that no other sport can compare, even remotely, with angling for educational value.

Persuasion
Perhaps the greatest service that any sport can do for a boy or a young man is encouraging him to read. There's a lot of difference between reading with ease, and being capable of deciphering the written or printed word. I know a good many teachers and they all agree that one of the most important aspects of education is persuading their pupils to read enough to be able to read easily and quickly.

What helps most is a desire by the pupil to find something out, and his realisation that books can tell him what he wants to know. Tell a boy to go home and read a chapter of Dickens, and usually he couldn't care less. He may go and read it, but he doesn't really want to know what it says. He does not feel that the information or the entertainment are of any value to him.

But let that boy be an angler, anxious to catch a big, fat chub. Hand him a book by Fred Taylor or Peter Stone and suggest he reads the chapter on chub fishing. You won't need to press him very hard. He'll read it! He'll read it several times. He'll read anything he can get hold of about fishing and he'll remember what he reads.

There won't be any shortage of reading material, either. There are about ten times as many books about fishing as about all other sports put together, and for the most part, the standard of English in these books is high. On top of that, there are plenty of angling periodicals.

So in this aspect of encouraging youngsters to read, angling stands far, far above any other sport.

Of course, as we all well know, angling has much more to offer in educational value. It is impossible to be a good all round angler without being a good naturalist. You need to know as much as you can about the fish themselves, their way of life, habits and behaviour. You need to know about their food, and that involves learning about insects, crustacea, molluscs, plants and other organisms.

If you fish, you can't avoid seeing a great deal of the wildlife at the waterside. You learn about all kinds of animals and birds from first-hand observation. You also learn something of drainage problems, water conservation, and often a good deal about farming, too.

Then there is craftsmanship. It is possible to fish without making a single item of tackle, but a few do and even they have to learn to tie proper knots. Many more become involved to a greater or lesser extent in various aspects of tackle making, be it making floats, plugs, flies, nets or even rods, and it is the younger angler who has the greatest incentive to do so.

In many schools, he receives sympathetic help in such enterprises from his craft teachers. And the more forward-looking teacher well appreciates that it is much easier to instruct a boy who is making something he wants to make, and wants to make well, than something about which he doesn't care a jot.

We are often told about the character-building effect of team games. How valid these claims are, I don't know. What I do know is that once a young fellow leaves school, his opportunity to participate in team games is usually very greatly reduced and, generally speaking, it is only those whose prowess is far above average who have much chance.

(pages 30-1) *The author and a young angler take time out for a technical discussion. No other sport can compare, even remotely, with angling for educational value*

29

Character

It doesn't take twenty-two people to go fishing, though. One can go fishing alone or with one or two friends, at almost any time one chooses. Don't tell me it doesn't involve exercise, either. Young anglers that I know walk and cycle tremendous distances for their fishing.

As for character building no sport equals angling for emphasising the value of observation, persistence, logical thinking and ingenuity. Non-anglers think we spend our fishing days sitting watching a float and catching nothing.

Haven't we all heard the dreary non-angling bore declaim: 'I've watched hundreds of anglers fishing but I never saw one catch a fish!' It never occurs to these dashing gentlemen whose idea of pulse-stirring excitement is usually something like wallowing around a gravel pit in a dinghy, or walking after a golf ball, or yelling at a professional footballer on a Saturday afternoon, that the main reason we seldom catch fish when they're wandering along the river bank is that they've scared every fish for miles.

We know better. We know that in fishing as in other sports, success has to be earned; but success in fishing demands more than skill of hand or athletic ability. It demands hard thinking and the building-up of useful knowledge. There aren't many subjects in a modern school that can't be of use to an angler, and some like maths, physics, biology and chemistry, can be of tremendous help.

I've said before and will say again that a young fellow who wants to be a successful angler cannot afford to neglect his school work. In angling, ignorance means failure, more than in any other sport.

Angling not educational? Ask any Probation Officer how many juvenile delinquents he has to deal with are anglers. Ask how many are rescued from deliquency by becoming interested in fishing.

Ask any schoolmaster who is an angler himself, whether or not he can use the fact that some of his pupils are anglers to aid his teaching immensely.

The fact is that fishing is a great educator, and it is a pity that more educationalists fail to realise it.

31 March 1967

Living with nature's 'anglers'

I'm often surprised at how little most anglers know about the birds and mammals that live at, or near, the waterside. So many appear to think that if wildlife eat fish, they're menaces, and if they don't they don't matter.

Let's have a look at some of the commoner birds, like the heron, crested grebe, kingfisher, dabchick, coot, and moorhen. The first three eat fish, the last three don't. Actually, a dabchick may occasionally catch and eat a very small fish, but it lives mainly on other things. Coots and moorhens don't eat fish at all.

Do herons, grebes and kingfishers harm angling? The answer, of course, is no, unless they get to work on a hatchery or stockpond, in which case the damage they can do is tremendous.

Herons live mainly on eels and small species of fish like gudgeon, loach and bullheads, though they'll also chomp frogs, mice or rats if they get the chance. Occasionally a heron manages to catch a trout of 1/2lb or so, and they will sometimes stab and injure bigger fish, but such instances are very rare. The overall picture is that by reducing the numbers of eels and small fish, herons are beneficial to angling waters.

The same applies to crested grebes. These wonderful divers eat little roach, rudd and bream. They can't cope with anything over about 5 inches long.

Kingfishers live almost entirely on minnows and other small fish of similar size. There's hardly a fishery that holds minnows that doesn't hold too many from the angler's point of view. The kingfisher should be welcome to all he can catch.

In passing, we might mention that rare bird, the bittern. He eats much the same sort of fish as the heron. Just hearing a bittern would make up for catching no fish all day, as far as I'm concerned.

A much more serious charge against these birds than what they eat is the part they may play in spreading fish diseases and parasites. Some of them feature in the life cycle of certain parasites like ligula; but these have serious effects on fish only when the environment has been unbalanced in some way, usually through the activities of man.

There are some other birds that are less desirable. When sea or

33

estuarine birds like cormorants, mergansers and goosanders take it into their heads to move into inland waters, they are capable of doing considerable damage to fisheries, more than their interesting characters can compensate.

It is easy to say that there must be a reason for their change of feeding grounds. By all means seek the reason, but a 12-bore may often be the immediate and sensible remedy.

There are many other interesting waterside birds and I can't hope to deal with all of them here, but there's one more to mention, the water rail. Although it isn't at all rare, few anglers see it because it is dead crafty about using cover and moving about.

That was why, when I began writing about fishing many years ago, and it was usual to use pen-names, I chose 'Water Rail' as mine. I've always believed in the importance of concealment, and I'd go so far as to say that an angler who often sees water rails has little to learn about being quiet and unobtrusive while he's fishing. The chap who's never seen one might do well to ask himself why!

Now what about the mammals? The obvious one to mention first is the otter, about which there is probably more nonsense talked than almost any other creature you could name. Artists paint it sitting on a rock in midstream, holding a big salmon under one paw. Otters almost never catch salmon and it would take a whole family of them to do it, and then only in conditions of extremely low water.

Otters are supposed to catch salmon after salmon, take a choice bite from the shoulder of each, and then leave the rest to rats and crows. This is the most complete rubbish. The only time an otter leaves a fish, on the rare occasions when he catches a sea-trout or small salmon, is when someone comes along the bank and scares him.

In fact, the otter is a most economical feeder. If he's given the chance and isn't scared off, all he leaves of his catch is a bit of slime on the grass from eels, which is what he mostly lives on, or a patch of scales from the occasional chub he catches. He never kills more than he needs; and of course like most other waterside creatures, he is of benefit to our fisheries. We would be better off with many more otters.

The otter is equipped by nature to hunt his main food, eels. The mink isn't, so he catches fish we'd like to catch. He can do a lot of damage to a fishery and to the smaller birds and animals that inhabit its banks.

Lots of anglers don't know the difference between a water rat, more correctly called a water vole, and a common brown rat. The water vole is a richer brown, more stockily built, and has a shorter furry tail. A brown rat has a bald, long, snaky tail.

The vole is vegetarian, a nice little chap whose only crime is that when he gets too numerous, he undermines river banks by his burrowing. The brown rat is an unmitigated, vicious pest, and it's a shame that so many water voles are killed in mistake for him. The brown rat is becoming more and more common as a waterside animal; it can dive and swim, below or at the surface, very expertly.

Another quite common but seldom seen animal is the water shrew. He too is a most expert swimmer, and a fierce and deadly hunter. The only thing that stops him eating you is that he isn't big enough. Otherwise he'd chomp you like a shot, as he does the loach, bullheads, minnows, gudgeon and other small fish he catches.

As it is, being smaller than a mouse handicaps him. I've sometimes wondered if water shrews ever look at Fred J. Taylor and think how tasty he'd probably be if only they were big enough to set about him.

Anglers vary in their interest in waterside creatures, but I think more and more are finding that studying them during fishing hours adds greatly to the interest of the day.

I once saw an osprey catch a dace from the Hampshire Avon. I can't remember what I caught that day, or even whether I caught any fish at all, but I shall remember the osprey all my life.

6 July 1967

Angling and astrology don't mix

Every now and then, a reader writes to ask me what I think of the Solunar theory.

This theory was first put forward by a famous angler John Alden

Knight. It holds that the feeding fish is governed by the relative positions of the earth, the moon and the sun.

That isn't quite the astrological nonsense that it seems at first because the sun and moon do produce tides, and in the sea the tide affects the feeding of fish.

The Solunar theory, however, holds that even in inland waters, where tides are imperceptible, fish are still affected. Lots of anglers in the United States seem to accept the idea to judge from the number of calendars that appear in their tackle catalogues and elsewhere, setting out which days are good and bad for fishing.

Since tackle manufacturers don't want to discourage anyone from going fishing at any time, it's amusing to see that these calendars often describe days in terms of good, very good and excellent, instead of good, not so good and bad!

Some years ago, my old friend Lewis Harris did a lot of investigation to determine whether or not there was any validity in the Solunar theory. I never heard from him whether he had reached a definite conclusion. But he encouraged me to look into the matter myself.

My view is that you are just as likely to make a good catch on those days the Solunar theory says are the worst you could choose, as on those days that the theory says are best. I don't believe that the feeding of freshwater fish is in the least bit affected by the gravitational pull of the moon or the sun.

Of course, that is not to say that the sun and moon have no affect at all. Fish eat less food in winter than in summer because temperatures are lower. Waters produce less food and the fish, because their metabolic rate is lower at low temperatures, need less and eat less.

The moon also has some affect, all through the year. On a day following a full or nearly full moon in a clear night sky, fishing is usually poor. I used to think that this was because a clear night sky always means low night temperature, through radiation loss. And so it does, but that isn't the whole story.

You can have a clear sky and low night temperatures when the moon is only a thin crescent, but the following day's fishing may be very good. I now think that it is the bright moonlight that does the damage.

Why, I don't really know. I've heard it said that fish feed all night in bright moonlight and then don't want any more food the next day. I can't accept this idea.

Fish often feed all night when the moon is the opposite of full, or so obscured by the clouds that the night is as dark as it can get. In fact, my experience is that the best kind of night for catching fish is a mild, but very dark one.

My record carp was caught on the darkest night I can remember, and I've taken many good fish on such nights, whereas bright moonlight nights have seldom produced good catches.

Nevertheless, these bright moonlit nights generally are followed by days on which fishing is poor. I don't say there aren't exceptions. There are always exceptions to any generalisations about fishing, but I never feel very confident about making a good catch on a day following a night of bright moonlight.

Many experienced anglers say that this is specially true of pike-fishing; that pike hardly ever feed after a moonlit night. I don't reckon myself as much of a pike-fisher, but such experience as I have agrees with what many experts claim.

Now I'm pretty sure that pike in Loch Lomond do most of their summer feeding either at night, or early in the morning. Their stomach contents invariably consisted of partly-digested powan.

Since we caught these pike between 11am and 9pm most days, the powan in their stomachs were swallowed several hours before the pike were caught. This puts their feeding time after 9pm and before about 6 or 7am. It seems reasonable to assume that this means at night or in the grey of the dawn, which ties up with another known fact.

The small organisms on which powan feed, things like daphnia and other tiny crustacea, move vertically according to the strength of the light. The brighter the light, the deeper they go. So at night, they're just under the surface. It seems logical that the powan, when feeding on these crustacea near the surface at night, are attacked by the pike from below.

The vertical migration of the tiny crustacea probably accounts for the phenomenon known as 'flipping', which is noticeable on some carp waters in the middle of dark nights.

Suddenly hundreds of little carp start splashing, swirling and sometimes actually leaping, at the suface. It goes on for anything from five minutes to perhaps half an hour. Then stops as suddenly

37

as it started. It seems likely that these little fish are feeding on daphnia, or other small crustaceans, that have moved up under the surface.

On lakes and reservoirs that hold trout and other fish, you some-times find the bigger trout feeding on small fry at the surface in the middle of the night. Here again, this is probably due to the small crustacea being there at that time, and attracting the small fry, on which the big trout feed.

Too little is known about how fish react for any definite conclu-sion to be drawn. But it may be at least in some waters, that a full migration of the small crustacea from bottom to top and back, triggers off the greatest feeding activity by fish of all sorts and sizes.

16 January 1969

Murderers who go free

'Let's treat pollution as a criminal offence!'

When, after World War II, trials were held for those accused of war crimes and atrocities, the usual plea was: 'Yes, I did it, but I was only obeying orders.'

This plea is not accepted in civilised countries, except, it seems, when the crime consists of murdering the wildlife that lives in and around rivers.

If the employee of a local authority or a large industrial company is told by his boss that he is to empty a filthy sewage tank, or dump a few pounds of cyanide into the nearest river, he does so cheer-fully. He cannot be prosecuted for it.

If his bosses aren't well represented on the river authority, a prosecution may result, but it won't be against him, or indeed any other individual. It'll be against the authority or the company who employs him, and if successful, the fine will be paid, if the offender is a local authority, out of public funds.

Consumer pays
If the offender is a nationalised industry, like the Coal Board, the Electricity Authority, or the Gas Board, then the fine will come

out of what the consumer pays – the public, in fact.

If it's a private or public company, the fine comes out of what consumers pay for the goods or services it supplies. The public, again, pays. Remember when the Trent River Authority prosecuted the Electricity Authority for a gross pollution of the River Trent? The prosecution was successful and the fine was £100.

Who paid the money? The Electricity Authority? No, electricity consumers. How many of them even knew they had done so? None, of course. Clearly neither the prosecution nor the fine had any effect whatever on anyone. All it did was waste time in court.

River authorities are, for practical purposes, absolutely powerless to curb pollution, except that caused by individual farmers and small firms. The big boys laugh at fines.

We shall never contain pollution through action by river authorities until we accept the principle that no man can escape responsibility by the plea that he was acting under orders. What we need is legislation that allows a river authority to call in the police to deal with an act of pollution as a criminal offence. The police should be provided with the specialised evidence necessary for a prosecution, not of a firm or a local authority, but of the person who actually put or let the poison into the river.

Stiff sentences

This legislation should provide for punishment that includes stiff prison sentences for bad cases. After all, polluting substances don't get into rivers of their own accord. They get in through either the positive act or the criminal negligence of some human being, who has a name and address and who, usually, can be traced easily enough.

If such individuals were well aware that if they put or allowed to get into a river, any substance that killed the inhabitants of that river, they stood a very good chance of finding themselves in jail for a year, we should soon find that very little pollution occurred.

There's one more thing we need and that is acceptance of the fact that more needs to be done than simply trying to stop matters getting worse. Many rivers have been virtually destroyed by source abstraction. Established abstractions of this kind are perfectly legal, provided they have been going on long enough.

In the vast majority of cases, such abstractions are not the only

A perfect natural river, offering the angler plenty of concealment and a variety of specimen fish. This stretch of Hertfordshire's River Oughton held trout to 4lb and a variety of big coarse fish when the picture was taken in the fifties

means for obtaining water. There's at least as much water at the downstream end of a river as there is at its source, and usually a lot more. The only reason why water is abstracted from the source is that it needs much less purification and is consequently cheaper.

Fully exploited

Not long ago the Lee Valley Water Company gave as one of its reasons for having to increase the water rate the fact that, as they said: 'All cheap local sources of water are now fully exploited.'

What they meant was that they were extracting nearly every

drop of water they could get from the sources of all Hertfordshire rivers and streams and some of the streams that run into Bedfordshire, into the bargain.

What we need is an Act of Parliament setting a time limit within which source abstraction must stop and alternative, albeit rather more expensive, sources of water found. Why should the general public get water a penny or two per thousand gallons cheaper, at the expense of ruining every river in their area and all that that involves?

I believe that if the facts about water supplies and source abstraction were well known to the public, most people would willingly pay a few shillings more for water supplies, if by doing so they could ensure that our rivers and streams could be restored to their former condition, before source abstraction commenced.

Health hazard

They would know that this isn't simply a matter of restoring the sport available to anglers. It goes much farther than that. All the birds and animals of these river and stream valleys are affected, and so is public health.

Whether these legislative changes that we need will ever be made, I don't know. It seems to me unlikely. Our major political parties seem to me to be committed to the policy that many historians think was responsible for the fall of the Roman Empire: panem et circenes, which means bread and circuses.

It's the philosophy of giving the public cheap food and plenty of synthetic entertainment. In our day and age this means good subsidies and half a million quid to encourage football, not as a sport but as a spectacle.

Believe me, despite a few protestations here and there, the Government and any future Government we may elect, doesn't want you and me to participate in sport, especially in a sport that happens to be inconvenient.

They'd much rather pack us all in a stadium, yelling our heads off, than have us spread out along the banks of lakes and rivers, even if a few trains, shops, and goalkeepers' heads happen to get smashed in the process.

Their attitude is exactly the same as it was in Rome a couple of thousand years ago. Who cares what happens to a few gladiators or goalkeepers, as long as the public is kept occupied?

Well, we elect 'em, don't we?

6 November 1969

Clarissa started something big

The death of the record carp in London Zoo has brought me a shoal of correspondence and this week I'd like to deal with some of the things that arise from this.

The first is the suggestion that the fish should never have been removed from Redmire Pool in the first place. It should have been returned, say many of my correspondents, either to breed and so up-grade the strain of carp, or else to give other anglers a chance to catch it, preferably after it had grown still larger.

I think these suggestions stem from the idea that the fish was some kind of unique freak. The truth is that at the time I caught the fish, there were many other carp in Redmire Pool that were bigger.

One or two were much bigger, and those of us who saw them decided that they were in the region of 60lb. Whether fish as large as that still inhabit the pool, I don't know, but when I caught my fish in 1952, I didn't expect it to continue as the record fish for more than another year or two, at most.

The reason why I gave 'Clarissa' to the Zoo – and I say 'gave', because that's what I did – were that I was determined not to kill it, but I knew full well that if I returned it, no one would believe that it really weighed as much as it did.

Even if it had been accepted at the time, you can bet that the present Record Fish Committee would have disqualified it by now!

I felt it to be important that the fish should be very fully authenticated, because at that time there were relatively few waters holding big carp, and anglers generally held the view that stocking with carp was a waste of time and money.

Carp were thought to take about 100 years to grow to large size, and to be next to impossible to catch when they had.

So I wanted a lot of people to be able to see, if they liked, a fish that had grown at a rate of 3lb a year and which it had been possible to catch, so that they would be encouraged to stock suitable waters with carp.

You may ask, why carp? Here is the answer.

Around that time there was an enormous expansion in gravel and sand extraction around large centres of population, because the building industry had not only to make good a lot of bomb damage, but also make good the loss of five years in which very little building had been possible. This extraction of sand and gravel provided a lot of wet pits, offering fishing facilities for the rapidly increasing number of anglers.

Our experience had shown that in many such pits, the growth rates of such fish as roach, rudd, bream and perch were quite poor.

Now, anglers may not all be out to catch fish, but the majority likes to feel that the possibility of hooking something really big is

present. It isn't much fun to sit pulling out a succession of very small fish and knowing there isn't a hope of catching anything bigger.

Some of us therefore thought that stocking such waters with carp would be a good idea, because carp are very good at growing to large size in conditions where other species can't. In a poor gravel pit, they won't put on 3lb a year, but they'll grow to over 10lb in a reasonable time.

Well, in the event, the presence of the record carp in the Zoo, there for all to see, did encourage clubs and other angling organisations to stock with carp, and we are now reaping the benefits.

Another important effect of the capture was its effect upon tackle design and sales. Only anglers of long experience understand how great the effect was.

Up to the time that fish was caught, the choice open to a coarse fish angler wanting to buy a rod was very limited indeed.

He could either buy a pike rod or one of two basic kinds of roach-rod, one of Spanish reed or whole cane with a stiff butt and middle, the other a shorter and more flexible rod, with a split cane middle and top.

I am sure that what was done in carp-fishing in the 1950s brought about the realisation that such a range was far too limited, and led eventually to the very much wider choice of tackle that we now have. In the early 1950s, there were very few tackle shops in which you would find eyed hooks for freshwater fishing on sale, or indeed any hooks larger than a no 6.

Legering was practically unknown, landing nets were completely inadequate in size, and there was nothing like the range of auxiliary tackle that is available now.

I never did think it mattered who caught the 44lb carp, or that whoever did deserved any great credit for it. I said at the time and have said many times since that I've caught many carp of less than half the size that were more difficult to tempt, to hook, to play and to land than that one.

I've also said that it was a matter of pure chance that the fish

Dawn has broken, a big carp splashes and the angler's hand hovers expectantly over the rod butt. Carp fishing and all its excitement, once restricted to a few venues and a handful of anglers, is now available to thousands

took my bait and not Pete Thomas's, which was identical to mine and lying on the bottom with about a yard between the two.

No, what was important was that the fish was caught by somebody at about that time; and having been caught, it was essential that its capture became widely known and believed.

I think it was important, too, that whoever did catch such a fish should have been trying to do it, because if the fish had been caught by accident, by someone legering for eels, or after bream, or something like that, it would have failed to demonstrate that an angler can set out to catch a big fish of a particular species and succeed.

Here again, not many of today's younger anglers realise what was the general attitude in angling up to the early 1950s. Then, the catching of big fish was commonly supposed to be a matter of pure luck.

You just fished away with a roach rod and float tackle, and hoped that one day an outsize fish would come along and take your bait, after which your luck might extend to saving your tackle from breakage.

Of course there are still plenty of people who think that is how it goes, but many of those who held that view in 1951 had changed their minds before 16 June 1953!

The other points my correspondents make are relatively unimportant. No I am not going to make an all-out attempt to catch an even bigger carp for the London Zoo, but in the very unlikely event of my doing so, I'd not expect the Zoo to pay me for it.

On the contrary, I am very grateful to the Zoological Society's employees for all the trouble they've taken.

Especially at the time of the capture and for so many years after, to look after a fish which, on account of its size, always presented a considerable problem to them. They did very well indeed to keep it alive for so long.

Yes, I do think there is still a good chance of the weight being beaten, and the number of waters from which a bigger fish may come is much larger now than it was in 1952.

17 June 1971

Clarissa has now been set up and is on display at Fred Buller's tackle and gun shop in Amersham, Bucks.

If I Won the Pools

Watching the news on TV the other day, I heard that some lucky chap had won six figures of money on the pools, and I expect that I was only one among millions who started thinking what I'd do if I ever got my hands on that sort of 'mazuma'.

This is what I'd do.

I'd engage a few people to search out a large lake, not less than 75 acres and preferably a lot bigger. A wet gravel pit would do nicely. It would have to have at least 100 yards of land all round it, and access to a good road, and it would need to be at least 5 miles from any sizeable village or town.

I'd buy it if I could.

Then I'd draw up plans and obtain planning permission to carry them out.

The first step would be to engage a contractor to re-shape the banks into a series of bays and promontories, each bay about 40 yards wide with promontories on each side extending out for 30 to 50 yards. About 15 yards from the inner shore of each bay I'd have a concrete slab, on which there would be a wooden chalet, with hard standing for a car beside it and a concrete track connecting it to a peripheral road that ran all the way round the lake.

The whole area would be plentifully planted with trees and shrubs, especially the promontories. They'd be so thick that an angler fishing in a bay would be quite unable to see other anglers fishing in adjoining bays, except right across on the opposite side of the lake.

The chalets would be small but comfortable, with electric heating and cooking facilities. There would be two built-in bunks and an arrangement of cupboards, fold down table and bench seats – rather as in a caravan; and a full complement of cooking utensils, plates, cups and cutlery.

The peripheral road would be strictly one-way only.

Near the entrance to the premises would be a large fishing lodge, which would house a general store, where anything an angler might want to buy during a week's stay would be available. Food, drinks, tobacco, tackle, bait, groundbait, film, various accessories and even petrol, would all be there.

As well as the store there would be a very comfortable lounge with a licensed bar, and there would be plenty of stuffed fish and good fishing photographs hung around the walls.

Definitely no radio or TV there, but portable TV sets would be available, on hire, for use in the chalets.

Comfortable

Each chalet would be numbered and in the bay adjacent to it, there would be moored a very comfortable punt, also numbered and provided with oars, a punting pole and two mooring poles. It would have a very capacious well, to avoid any need for keepnets, and under the decking at each end would be a big buoyancy compartment filled with expanded polystyrene.

Each punt would also be provided with a coloured and numbered marker buoy, a rope and weight, for marking baited swims.

Weed-drags would be available on request from the fishing lodge, though, enough weed cutting would be done by the management, through the season, to ensure plenty of room for fishing.

The lake would be stocked with coarse fish on the advice of an expert like Eric Birch. The species most suitable for the particular water would be selected and everything possible done to ensure that big catches would be made and that plenty of specimen fish figured in those catches.

I should want to engage a married couple, someone like Mr and Mrs Ernest Leah, to supervise things generally. They would have some help in the form of three or four young men, for whom I'd like to make whatever arrangements I could in the way of educational opportunities in fishery management and fish farming; probably by long visits to parts of Europe where the right facilities are available.

Of course, the contractors engaged to shape the lake would also have dug out a series of stock-ponds capable of being drained independently, where suitable species could be bred and fed to good size before being released.

Modest

Fishing would be arranged on the simple basis of letting chalets, at so much for Monday to Friday inclusive and so much for Saturday and Sunday.

The letting fee, which would include fishing, would be very modest indeed because I should expect to make my profit not on the letting of the chalets, fishing and use of punts, but on what anglers spent on other things while on the premises.

Yes, I should set out to make a good profit! Enterprises that make losses don't last long. In fact, I should aim for a profit that would allow me, in a few years, to start looking for another water where the whole process could be repeated.

Simple

Rules for fishing would be quite simple. The two anglers who booked a hut would have the exclusive right to fish from any point on the bank round the adjacent bay, or anywhere from the punt, provided they went no nearer to another angler or one of the numbered buoys than 50 yards.

That would ensure that a pair of anglers who baited a swim would have the sole use of it during their stay. Of course parties of more than two would be able to fish together if they wished and to book adjacent chalets.

At the fishing lodge, a very large map of the lake would be displayed on the wall, with each bay and chalet numbered and a cuphook screwed in, bearing a numbered disc.

As chalets were booked, the appropriate discs would be removed by the management, ready to hand to each pair of anglers on arrival. Any discs remaining on the board at any time would be available to anglers already booked in, by calling at the office, so that bays not booked could be fished if anyone wanted to do so.

There would be very few other rules for fishing. The whole aim of the enterprise would be to provide the best coarse fishing that could be contrived in a comfortable and friendly atmosphere, and at as low a cost as was consistent with profitability.

There is a good profit to be made in providing people with what they would have needed to buy, even if they'd stayed at home.

Well, I haven't the kind of money that would be needed for such a scheme. But it's a pleasant thought to dream up such a situation.

23 December 1971

Don't allow yourself to be brainwashed

In the recent debate about the usefulness of match tackle for general fishing, I noticed that I appear to be regarded as a specimen hunter. It made me wonder what a specimen hunter is and whether I am one.

It is easy enough to define a matchfisher – someone who takes part in organised attempts to see who can catch most fish in a specified time. Defining a specimen hunter isn't so easy.

You can say he is an angler who set out to catch specimen fish, but then you have to say what you mean by a specimen fish. And there is where you run into all kinds of trouble.

As I grow older, the world seems to me to be filled with earnest young men who share the ambition to set new records. Depending upon just how serious they are about this, they are dooming themselves to almost inevitable disappointment.

There is a legend about some Sussex villagers who, seeing the moon's reflection in the local pond, thought it was a floating cheese and tried to extract it with rakes. Setting out to break angling records is rather like that.

Fishing records are unlike any other kind, for a variety of reasons. Other records are always breakable. If you have ambitions to set a new record for the 1,500m, there is always 1,500m to run. There isn't always a record fish to catch. The late Reverend Edward Alston's 4½lb rudd holds the record for that species. Who can say where and if a bigger rudd can be found today? The same applies to many other species.

Nor is the capture of a record fish anything about which to boast. An exceptionally big fish is of biological interest and little more. Its capture says nothing about the ability of the angler who caught it. Many a record fish has been caught by an angler of very limited ability, and even when we consider record fish that were caught by intent rather than by accident, we can still never say their captors were proved thereby to be exceptionally good anglers.

I am writing this because I am one of the few who can do so without my motives being questioned. I happen to have broken some records. Let's consider just one – and readers of long standing

The author and his life-long angling companion, Pete Thomas, pictured together on the Upper Ouse at Beachampton

will, I hope, forgive me for repeating what I said about it some years ago, because I think it needs repeating from time to time.

In June 1952, Pete Thomas and I were fishing together. He caught a carp of 28lb 10oz, the second biggest ever taken at that time. I caught two small carp, about 5lb each. Nobody assumed that this proved Pete to be a better angler than I.

In September of that year, I caught a 44lb carp. Pete who was with me, caught nothing. This did not make me a better angler than Pete. It was pure chance that led the fish to take my bait and not his. Our baits were identical and lying close together.

Here's another thing. Nobody really knows, or ever will, what that fish actually weighed. There's no doubt about what it weighed when it arrived at Regent's Park, because it was put on scales checked at the time by an Inspector of weights and measures and certified as accurate. But it might have weighed more when first landed. A fish of that size can vary in weight by a pound or two from day to day, because it can easily eat, or excrete, that much.

I tend to chuckle when I read that someone has caught a fish weighing, let's say, 11lb 3oz 5dr. What are the 3oz and the 5dr all about? They're meaningless, of course. I turn that fish loose, catch it again in a week, and it could weigh anything between 10 and 12lb. Recaptures of carp and pike that could be positively identified prove how much variation there can be between one time of capture and another. The whole exercise, when you come to think of it, is pretty silly.

If the simple system we have for records is silly, what can we say about the American idea of line-class records? They have a whole range of records for each species, based not only on fish weights but also on the strength of the tackle on which the fish were caught. The idea appears to be that the finer the line on which a fish was caught, the more creditable is the capture.

It leads to some comicalities, because at one end of the scale, you can sometimes find a quite modest-sized fish that holds a line-class record not because it was caught on a very fine line, but because it was taken on a very strong one. I am wondering if I can claim the 12lb line class for roach, having caught one or two roach between 2lb and 3lb on a 15lb line, entirely by accident while fishing for carp.

The trouble is that the public have been brainwashed into worshipping records and round figures.

It has become the same in fishing. An angler catches a roach. Looks as if it might go to 2lb. With bated breath he watches the scales: 2lb 1oz, joy unabated . . . 1lb 15oz, stark misery!

Happy is the angler who is content to catch a fish big enough to put up a good fight and to need a landing net to put it on the bank, without caring a damn whether it is bigger or smaller than another fish of the same kind that someone else has caught, or if it happens to weigh some arbitrary round figure of pounds or kilograms or whatever other units of weight may be in vogue.

If pursuing records or round figures is specimen hunting, I'm not a specimen hunter. If it means enjoying catching a few fish that have grown out of the tiddler class and got big enough to break me if I'm not careful, then perhaps I am.

19 March 1980

We must defend our sport

Until fairly recently, anglers were regarded by the great majority of the public as harmless and slightly eccentric. We could afford to smile at the remarks about anglers growing longer arms so that they could lie more convincingly, and all the rest of the antique music-hall jokes.

Not any more. There is now an organised and growing campaign against angling. More and more people are being persuaded that angling is a vicious and cruel sport that ought to be banned by law.

Only recently, a letter appeared in my local paper, written by a lady whose main concern, which I sympathise with, was the killing of whales. She did however, accuse anglers of causing agonising deaths to fish. She is not alone in this mistaken belief.

More and more people with urban backgrounds, who know nothing about fishing, are being convinced that we are sub-humans who revel in torturing innocent fish to death and in poisoning swans by feeding them with lead shot or in tangling birds of all sorts in nylon monofil.

Every sensational accusation, however ill-founded or unsupported by real evidence, is seized upon by the press, radio and TV, exaggerated and served up to the public as proven fact.

So effective is this campaign that even some anglers are convinced by it. Letters from anglers have appeared in which it has been stated that thousands of swans have been killed by swallowing lead shot.

Many anglers feel secure in the belief that too many people are involved in our sport for any government to take measures against it. I am not so complacent. Action against us does not necessarily come from central government.

Banned

There are already many local councils who have banned fishing on waters under their control – without opposition there will be many more. The battle is already on and we must be ready to defend ourselves.

The way to do it is to keep watch, all the time, for any attacks in the media and to counter them by the facts. We may not convince the instigators of these attacks, but we can at least minimise their effect upon the public.

This we can do by answering the attacks whenever and wherever possible, either by writing letters for publication where the attacks appear in newspapers, or by complaining to other media about any distortions we may notice.

Those of us who do not feel competent to answer the attacks can at least draw attention to them by contacting club secretaries or the NAC or the British Field Sports Society.

For those who can write, I have some advice. Never cast doubt in a letter, on the sincerity of our attackers. Ignorant and misguided as they are, they do believe in what they write – except for a minority who rejoice in causing trouble, usually for political ends.

Nor should anyone try to divert attacks on angling towards other sports. It has been all too common in the past for foxhunters, hare coursers and others, when under attack, to take the line, 'Why pick on us, when angling is much more cruel?'

This is no argument whatever; it only causes division and provides extra ammunition for our enemies.

If angling is under attack, it must be defended on its own merits. Letters must be short and to the point. Here is an example – the letter I wrote in answer to the lady who equated anglers with whalers and accused us of causing agonising deaths to fish. It was published in full without alteration in the local newspapers in which her letter appeared.

Astonished

'While I share Carole Piller's concern for the conservation of whales, I am astonished at her ignorance of angling. To compare the fate of a harpooned whale with that of a fish caught with rod and line is perfectly ridiculous.

'In the latter case, the fish feels no more than a pinprick – in a mouth that is relatively insensitive – to judge from the hard, sharp and prickly creatures that fish often eat.

'Anglers take considerable care to see that the fish they catch do not suffer. In the case of all but one or two species, the fish are returned alive and unharmed to the water. The exceptions, chiefly trout and salmon, are killed instantly by a sharp rap on the head.

No other creature killed to provide food is dispatched as mercifully and quickly as a fish killed by an angler.

'The fish that do suffer agonising deaths at the hands of an unthinking public are those that are all too often destroyed by pollution. But for the fight that anglers constantly wage against this evil, there would be very few fish in Britain.'

It is important, in answering attacks on angling, to know the facts. If you don't know those that apply to a particular attack, you can discover them by writing or telephoning the NAC, or the BFSS.

For example, a recent RSPCA commission reported that it had been shown that fish can feel pain. This was promptly seized upon by the media, their conclusion being that fishing was, therefore, cruel.

The evidence came from a single scientist who had nothing whatever to say about the real issue, which is whether the fish feel pain when caught by rod and line.

The fact is that there is ample evidence to show that they do not. Their mouths are insensitive to sharp objects, otherwise they could not eat such things as sticklebacks, crayfish, water snails, mussels, or caddis in their cases made of sharp edged stones. Nor could they exert a pull on the angler's line, if the hook caused pain.

You can lead a 2-ton bull anywhere with a finger through the ring in his nose, but a fish can and often does pull hard enough to break quite a strong line.

The reason, of course, is that the bull's nose is sensitive to pain – the mouth of a fish is not. It is facts such as these that can be used to answer attacks on angling.

I mentioned earlier the lack of wisdom in trying to divert attacks on angling to other field sports, but there is nothing wrong, if space allows, in pointing out that anglers, including young anglers, do not indulge in street rioting, football hooliganism, train wrecking, vandalism or drug addiction.

Enemies

Nor is there any reason for refraining from pointing out that the real enemies of fish are not anglers but such evils as pollution, abstraction, backfilling of pits and vandalistic dredging, all of which damages not only fish but the whole ecology of rivers, lakes and other bodies of water. These are evils that anglers have been fighting for years.

It is a pity that the anti-angling lobby, which professes to be concerned about the welfare of fish, does nothing whatever to combat those influences that seriously diminish our fish population, and, incidentally, subject fish to really painful deaths.

It is sad but true, that when emotion and ignorance walk hand in hand through the door, truth usually flies out of the window. Only lately, an official of the RSPCA announced that great numbers of swans were being killed by swallowing lead shot in many areas.

What is the truth? It is that a few hundred swans have died of lead poisoning over the last six or seven years – all, or nearly all, of them in a few areas where heavy concentrations of powered pleasure craft are operated.

The population of swans nationwide has remained almost constant and such small reductions that have occurred are much more likely to be due to destruction of nesting sites by dredging or by the wash of large powered vessels driven at excessive speeds.

So there it is. The battle is on and if we wish to retain our right to fish we must defend it positively and not just sit back and rely on our numbers. Many a tiny army has defeated a much larger one. Let us not lose our sport for that reason.

1 September 1983

Here's my reply to people who are unable to accept my points of view . . .

A few weeks ago, a letter from a reader was published in *Angling Times* which accused me of being out of touch with the average angler and of advocating archaic methods of fishing.

What this had to do with the subject under discussion, which was whether anglers should support other fieldsports, I didn't understand. But if these comments were meant to provoke a rise from me, like a well-chosen trout fly, they have succeeded.

Long time

I've been fishing for a very long time, during which I've never met either an average angler or an expert. The longer I fish, the more I realise how much remains to be learned. But, far from being out of touch with anglers generally, I doubt if anyone else answers more letters, ranging from ten-year-old schoolboys to university professors, barristers and other professional men, than I do.

I have long since abandoned false modesty, and there's an old saying that if you don't blow your own trumpet, nobody else will blow it for you. So this week, I'm going to blow mine, by asking some questions. Here they come!

Who wrote the first book about stillwater fishing, with special reference to the problems of catching specimen fish?

Satisfactory

Who designed and built the first satisfactory carp rod and has been designing carp rods, in cane at first, then fibreglass, and now in carbon fibre, with calculated tapers, ever since?

Who designed and made the first net big enough to hold a 50lb fish, yet light enough to be used with one hand?

Who invented the electric bite alarm?

Who invented the Arlesey bomb, now to be found in nearly every coarse fish angler's tackle box?

Who devised the combination of paste and crust that produced a slow-sinking bait that would come to rest on silkweed or soft mud?

Who invented vanes, like dart flights, for float tops, visible at long range and able to make use of the wind to take a bait to the right place? These vanes are now used by many pike fishers.

Invented

Who invented a type of rod rest that ensured that the line would not be trapped between the rod and the rest?

Who pointed out, again and again, that fixed-spool reels needed rotating pick-up rollers, at a time when not one production reel was so fitted?

Who campaigned for knotless keepnets, year after year, until Mr C. J. Field pioneered their commercial introduction, with the result that they are not only in universal use, but in most areas compulsory?

Who invented the single and double Grinner knots, superior to any other kind of knot for joining nylon line?

Who was first to detect the 'vibration' bite from barbel, as different from the simple rod-bending pull, and explain how to detect it?

Who, after hearing that a former colleague, Mr Leslie Phillips, at the Royal Aircraft Establishment at Farnborough, had invented carbon fibre, went racing down there with Jim Hardy, of Hardy Brothers, to see how this new material might be used in fishing rods?

Who was the first angler in the world to catch trout on a carbon fibre rod?

Who, after experimenting with a wide variety of different ways of joining hooks in tandem trout lures, finally discovered the best and easiest, namely a treble plait of 12lb nylon monofil?

Thorough

Who made a thorough investigation of the causes of loss of strength in nylon monofil, and discovered that it is due to either the effect of ultra-violet light, bright sunshine, or to wet oxidation, or both, refuting makers' claims that monofil was rot-proof?

Who discovered that the cracking of PVC coatings of modern fly lines was due to loss of plasticiser, brought about by a variety of factors including heat, the use of ordinary greases, or simply time in storage? Who devised a special grease to restore lost plasticiser?

Who, with the aid of expert chemist Arnold Neave, devised a dip-in liquid that would thoroughly impregnate and waterproof dry trout flies, consisting of silicone and suitable wax in a solvent, and which didn't alter the colours of the fly?

Valuable

Who, year after year, kept insisting that legering was a valuable method for the matchman, at a time when float-fishing was considered the only method worth using, and predicted that the day

Not the largest barbel ever caught by the author, but angling can still be enjoyable, even when the fish are small!

would come when the National Championship would be won with leger – and was proved right?

Who first advocated the streamlined float with a central tube to allow its use as a slider, instead of the then universal cork bung with slit and peg? And illustrated it in a book published thirty years ago?

Who, in the same book, described the running paternoster, now more commonly called the link leger – and illustrated it?

Who first described and advocated, for some conditions, the method now known as 'freelining'?

Who first explained how modern glass or carbon fibre rods could be broken by violent efforts to make such rods flex against their own slight weight, without sufficient load, in the form of either lead or fly-line on their tips?

Who explained that if you halve the thickness of a line, it becomes sixteen times more flexible, and vice-versa?

Who popularised the use of betalights in floats and other bite-indicators? Fair enough, I know Peter Wheat was the first in the field, but his efforts failed because the betalights used were too feeble by far. It was left to someone else to point out that a cheap betalight float that can't be seen beyond 5 to 7 yards is a poor buy; better to spend a few pounds more for one that you can see at thirty yards or more!

Who explained to the tackle trade that centrifugal governors on multiplier reels were the wrong way round; that instead of adding extra braking as the spool speeded up, they should add it as the spool slowed down?

I leave readers to answer these questions and to decide how many of them have the same answer!

As for archaic methods, well, fish don't change in less than millions of years. If I fail to advocate the use, for example, of a range of fifty different carp baits involving organic chemicals and proteins, it is because I know that carp will eat almost anything unless experience has taught them that certain baits are dangerous.

26 January 1983

PART II
BAITS AND GROUNDBAITS

Big baits for big fish

I've just had a letter from a reader who had several things to say that I think would be of general interest, and I wish I could find space to deal with them all.

The thing that really shook me in this letter was his reference to what he called my 'campaign against tiddler-snatching'.

I wonder if I shall ever succeed in convincing readers of *Angling Times* that I'm not conducting a campaign against tiddler-snatching.

Poor chances

As far as I'm concerned, anybody who wants to snatch tiddlers is welcome to do so. What's more, if I'm fishing in a match, as I am now and then, in conditions such that the chances of catching bigger fish are poor, I get busy snatching tiddlers as hard and fast as I can.

What I am concerned about is the large number of anglers who wrongly imagine that tackle and techniques that are suitable for tiddler-snatching are also suitable for catching specimen fish.

Any angler who has become successful at catching relatively small fish, and who now wants to catch some really big ones, has first of all got to shake off some bad habits, and then go in for a radical change in his outlook, his tackle, his tactics, his times and his baits.

His approach

And I will willingly agree that the successful hunter of specimen fish generally needs to change his approach quite as much if he decides to compete in matches.

What I want to emphasise is that the same methods will not succeed in both branches of angling.

Another point my correspondent makes is about maggots. He says, rightly, that maggots provide an easily obtained combined hook-bait and groundbait, easy to use and requiring no preparation; and while he agrees that there may be better baits for various kinds of fishing, especially where specimen fish are concerned, he'd like to know what they are and more about them.

Before dealing with other baits, let's consider the drawbacks of maggots as well as their advantages. The main objection to maggots is that they demand the use of a small hook which isn't strong enough to cope with big fish that need holding firmly to keep them out of weeds and snags.

Putting a bunch of maggots on a big hook is not a complete answer to the problem. If you groundbait extensively with maggots, you'll often find that the fish will take a single maggot, perhaps two maggots, but the more you put on, the fewer bites you'll get, a big bunch being refused altogether.

Even in conditions where a small hook is adequate, a single maggot is a small bait, one that can be taken as easily by a small fish as by a big one.

Since little fish are far more numerous, far more active, and much harder to scare than big fish, the law of averages is all against the angler trying to catch big fish on little baits – except in certain circumstances, exceptions rather than rules, when only big fish are in the chosen swim.

The maggot is a very useful bait, invaluable to the angler who understands when and when not to use it, but a handicap and a curse to the man who uses nothing else.

For all-round big-fish hunting, I place the maggot third in my list of important baits. Ahead of it come worms and bread.

Regrettably, worms are liable to prove expensive and uncertain in supply if you try to buy them nowadays. The town-dweller who has no garden is faced with quite a problem if he wants a regular supply of lobworms.

There is room for more enterprise in this matter of lobworm supplies. Golf green-keepers, park-keepers and groundsmen have plenty of worms. They put in a lot of work trying to get rid of them. Someone should tell them that they could augment their incomes by selling their unwanted lobs.

But bread is no problem for anyone. You can get an enormous amount of bread for the price of a gallon of maggots. More than you'd care to carry far. Four loaves will go a long way on most waters.

You can fish crust, flake, paste, balanced paste and crust, crust cubes, crumb cubes, big baits, little baits, all out of a loaf of bread, and make up your groundbait too, loose, medium or heavy, just as you wish.

Big fish can manage big baits. A 20lb carp will make short work of a tangerine-sized ball of paste

Some figures

I haven't kept exact records of all the good fish I've caught and I can't find sufficiently complete information about catches made by other people, but here are some figures in support of the confidence I have in worms and bread as baits.

I've caught 36 perch over 3lb, of which 34 were caught on lobworms.

My best twelve carp average 20lb, and all but two were caught on bread.

My best six tench were all caught on bread, and all I've ever caught over 4½lb were taken on either bread or worms.

I've never caught a bream over 5lb (and I've had more than I can remember over that weight) on anything but bread or worm.

I know maggots have accounted for some big bream, but nearly, if not quite all, the double-figure fish on record fell to worms or paste.

I've caught far more roach over 2lb, on crust or worm than on other baits. Even dace over 1lb haven't all fallen to maggots; in fact, of the seven I've had to date, three were on fly, two on small red worms and two on maggots.

Frog bait
Far more of the chub over 5lb I've caught were taken on lobworms than on other baits though my best two were caught on frogs.

Rudd are the exception; maggots have accounted for most of the fish upwards of 2lb that I've caught – but worms and bread are both excellent baits for big rudd.

I know no better bait for crucian carp than small red worms, unless it's a bit of new flake from a loaf of bread.

One word of warning. In waters that are fished by large numbers of anglers, most of whom throw in large quantities of maggots, it is often difficult to catch fish on anything else.

Wherever fish are continually pelted with large numbers of small food particles, they are liable to refuse bigger baits.

That is not the fault of the baits, nor does it mean that the principle of using big baits for big fish is at fault. It is the collective action of the anglers that is wrong.

20 July 1956

The wrong sort of groundbait can actually rob you of fish

I have come to the conclusion that the least understood part of angling is the art of groundbaiting. What's more, until a year or two ago, I didn't know much about it myself.

I began to learn when I was asked to help devise a groundbait mixture that would serve for all kinds of coarse-fish angling. I thought it would be easy. How wrong I was!

In the past, I'd made up groundbait on a very hit-and-miss basis, using whatever wholesome meal happened to be available, and adding some other kind of meal if necessary.

For example, in lakes and canals I might use fine breadcrumbs or biscuit meal. For faster water, I'd add a bit of barley meal to stiffen it, or failing that, some pure flour. Often, I'd use soaked, mashed-up bread, with or without bran added.

I had a lot of faith in bread and bran for fast water at one time. I lost it however, when a river-keeper friend made up a sack of groundbait for me. There must have been fifty firm, heavy balls of it, each as big as a cricket ball or bigger.

I threw one in. It hit the water with a satisfying 'bloomph' and disappeared. I turned to pick another, and looked round again just in time to see the first bob up to the surface. We watched it go down the river, till it disappeared from sight round a bend.

Subsequent experiments showed that the amount of bran you can add to bread groundbait without making it too light, is so little that it's hardly worth adding it at all. For really fast water, even pure bread groundbait is not heavy enough.

Some tests

It can be made heavier with barley meal or by using newer bread, and that's the way I used to use it in heavier water, until I got asked to help with this proprietary bait. When you're involved in something that fellow anglers are going to pay for, you feel responsible. Your own groundbait can only affect your own fishing, but any sold in quantity can make or mar the sport of many. So I did some tests.

They showed that my bread and barley-meal, or new-bread mix, were pretty poor. In fact, they were worse than useless in many swims. I found this out by dropping balls of groundbait over a bridge, into clear water. They sunk all right, and at first everything was fine. A nice trail of particles washed off, and soon fish began to work up to where the balls of groundbait lay.

But soon the balls began to break up. All at once, a ball would disintegrate into smaller lumps, and there would be anything from ten to forty or more of these. The lumps wouldn't hold bottom. Away they went down the river, and away went the fish after them.

Fast swims

No wonder I'd been getting long biteless spells when fishing similar fast swims in the past! My groundbait had been attracting fish

The author prepares to groundbait his chosen swim. Correct groundbait and groundbaiting is essential to attract and hold fish (D. Nash)

for ten minutes or so, but after that it had been actually taking them away again.

Well I'd learned something. We wanted a mixture that would be heavy enough to hit bottom and hold together while sinking, but which would continue to give off a fine cloudy trail until it was all, or nearly all, washed away, instead of breaking up into smaller lumps. And for commercial purposes, it had to be made up from readily-available wholesome meals.

We tried sausage rusk, which has the advantage of swelling up considerably when wetted, unlike biscuit meal. Rusk was too light, so we added flour. That made it stick beautifully, but it wouldn't wash-down properly, and hardly any cloud came off it.

There was a lot of puzzling and brain-racking at this stage. Then we did some tests on the rate at which various meals absorbed water, as well as on how much they could take up. We found that some, like rice flower and fine semolina, took it up very slowly, swelling as they did so. And that knowledge went a long way towards solving the problem.

We mixed rice flour and semolina, two meals with different take-up rates, but both slow, with sausage rusk and flour. When damped and squeezed into balls, not using too much water, the last two ingredients took up most of it. It wasn't until the ball of groundbait reached the bottom that there was any more for the rice and semolina to absorb, and that was coming from the outside of the ball, soaking inwards.

More water
The rice and semolina grains nearest the outside got it first. They swelled, and pushed off a little of the outside of the ball, which the current washed downstream in a cloud of fine particles. Now the next layer of slow take-up grains got more water.

So it went on, until all the ball of groundbait was washed away.

It was a revelation, looking down from that bridge and seeing it work. First a few dace arrived, then more and more. Then a shoal, some big ones among them. Then a trout; after that three or four medium-sized chub. Within half an hour there was a great black triangle of fish of all sorts and sizes attracted by those balls of groundbait, and still they came. No breaking away to follow big lumps of groundbait going downstream. There weren't any.

So far, so good. We had a good fast-water groundbait. What about slow and still water?

The first thing to try was more water and less squeezing; and that was all that was needed, or nearly so. Used so, the groundbait broke up as it hit the water and spread well. But there was a surprise. The slow-absorbing ingredients sank much more slowly. Some hardly sank at all; instead tiny white specks spread over a wide area. And they attracted fish from that wide area, to the place where the bulk of the groundbait had sunk.

The back of the problem was now broken, but quite a lot of experimenting was needed to get the best proportions for each of the four kinds of meal, and we added another ingredient to give the mixture an even more attractive mealy smell.

Of course there was a lot of testing in practical fishing to make sure the stuff really was effective. There we made some mistakes.

Sometimes we used too little, sometimes too much. Sometimes we put a lot in all at once when it would have been better to use it little and often. Sometimes we went wrong the other way round.

But we found out in the end that it worked beatifully when we used it right. No groundbait can do an angler's thinking for him. Unless he uses it correctly, it won't help a bit. We also found that if you kneaded up the mix, it made an excellent paste.

After all that, if anybody tells me that there is no advantage in using groundbait, or that the sort of groundbait you use isn't very important, I shan't believe them.

Whether you buy proprietary groundbaits or mix your own is up to you; but don't run away with the idea that a single cheap meal, or a haphazard mixture of cheap meals, will be as good as a properly-worked-out mixture, with the correct meals weighed out in the right proportions, because it won't.

Correct use

In fact, the wrong groundbait can actually rob you of fish you might have caught. It is this fact that leads many anglers to think that there's no advantage in groundbaiting. If it's the wrong groundbait, these anglers are right.

The right groundbait, however, correctly used, can increase catches enormously.

11 February 1966

Odd baits our fathers used

I enjoyed reading the account of the angler who had used woodlice very successfully as a bait for roach. Many years ago, I used them on the Lea and on some of its tributaries, and did very well with them. We used to call them sowbugs, and there are two kinds.

Actually, I'm no expert on these little creatures and for all I know there may be dozens of species, but when I used to collect them from under the bark of rotten trees, and such places, I found one sort that could roll into a ball and another, flatter sort, that couldn't.

Both can be used as bait, but I always did much better with the flat sort, and it isn't difficult to see why. This sort of woodlouse looks almost exactly like the very common freshwater louse *Argulus*, which is eaten freely by most kinds of fish.

I found out about woodlice as baits from my grandfather and I remember he was very fussy about fishing them on hooks of the right colour. He used to shake-up blued hooks in a can containing fine sand and water with some ordinary washing soda dissolved in it.

The hooks came out a sort of greyish colour, but whether they were grey immediately after the shaking or after a few days, I'm not sure. I do know that they were grey when the old chap came to use them, and matched the colour of the woodlice very well. They had to be sharpened again after the shaking in the sand, because that dulled their points.

I can also remember the size, No 13. They used bigger hooks forty years ago and No 13 was a great favourite with roach anglers. Whether insistence on hook colour was general then or only confined to my grandfather and his fishing mates, I don't know, but they made a great to-do about it.

Hooks for fishing crust, or what they called golden flake, had to be gilt. They felt very much handicapped if they hadn't got gilt hooks for those baits, so much so that they'd rather choose some other bait to suit what hooks they had.

Golden flake, by the way, takes some preparing. You take a very sharp knife and slice off a very thin layer of the bottom crust of a loaf, exposing a brighter layer. Then you take another thin slice, not deep enough to reach the white crumb. Cubes cut from this layer are golden flake.

Some anglers preferred to take crust of the same stratum from other areas of the loaf, of coarser texture and with bigger holes or 'bubbles' in it, and there were great debates about which was best, but none about what hook should be used to fish it. A No 13 gilt hook, and no other!

For hempseed, they often used the same sized hook, but it had to be bronzed, with its shank painted white. Sometimes they used a smaller hook, but the white shank was a must. Fishing hempseed meant loading with lead wire instead of shot, because roach took round shot in mistake for grains of hemp.

Grandfather had tackles made up on a huge winder, and not content with using lead wire instead of shot on his hemp tackle, he painted the coil of wire green. He hated using new, bright shot on any tackle, and used to soak all his shot and leads in vinegar to get rid of the shine.

Leads were invariably painted in various shades of green and brown. The paint got knocked off pretty quickly in fishing, of course, and I don't believe for a moment that while it was still there, it made any difference; but these old fellows were determined to do everything possible to increase their chances.

For fishing worms, they used bronzed or blued hooks with the whippings of red silk. Worm hooks had to be round bends. They wouldn't dream of using a worm on a crystal hook. If they changed from flake to worm, they wound the tackle they'd been using back on to the tackle winder, complete with float. Then they tied on another tackle, with the appropriate worm-hook at the end of it.

They took immense care in putting a worm on the hook. First they dipped their fingers in a little bag or tin of sand, so as to be able to grip the worm firmly. The hook point had to go into the worm and not come out again until the worm was threaded on sufficiently far; and that was when the whole of the shank and a bit of the gut was well inside that worm. If the point came out too soon, grandfather would swear, throw the worm away and start with a fresh one.

It was when he came to use caddis grubs that the swearing was at its worst. Caddis grubs were favourite in the first couple of weeks of the coarse fishing season, for catching roach and dace in the smaller rivers, which in those days ran quite fast and clear and held splendid fish. Rivers like the Beane and the Rib, which are now quite destroyed by water abstraction.

For caddis you used a special hook, a gilt round bend specially fine in the wire and the art was to thread the caddis on this without bursting it. The point had to go in at the exact spot at the rear end of the caddis and come out again between its little legs. If it went in or came out anywhere else, the caddis burst and then it was considered useless as a bait.

I, being then about 10 or 11 years old, had the job of collecting the caddis and I became very good at it. There are many different kinds living in different places. A very good sort favours the

71

feathery underwater roots of bankside willow trees. Its case is of dark bits of stick, snail shells and little stones, and the grub is golden yellow.

Another kind lives in a round stone house that is stuck permanently to stones in the fast shallow water. This is a green grub, quite small, but deadly for roach and dace fished on a size 16 hook. There are other sorts too like the caddis of the Great Red Sedge that makes a spiral sort of case out of bits of weed-stalk and lives among the thick weeds, so that it is hard to see.

Sometimes these old chaps fished with silkweed as bait. Need I tell you what colour the whipping was that held the hook to the gut? Yes, green. Either they whipped on their own hooks with green silk, or else they painted the whippings of bought hooks-to-gut with green paint.

They always told me that fish eat green silkweed because of the tiny snails, larvae and so on, that it contained. I didn't believe it then and I don't believe it now, because I could never find any snails, larvae or any other small creature, in the silkweed on the weir aprons. Fish eat silkweed for its own sake, and in high summer, they're often stuffed with it.

You don't need a green hook shank to catch them with it, either; but perhaps if you're keen enough to paint your hook-shank to match your bait, you'll end up with the better catches, not because of the colour of the hook-shank but because the attitude that leads to painting it green had also led to better overall efficiency in your angling.

Perhaps, before we had nylon and fibreglass and fixed-spool reels and all the modern improvements, the final touches of ultra-fussiness made more difference than they do now. Of one thing I am sure, fishing held far greater interest to these old chaps than it does to the host of modern anglers who hardly think it worth going fishing if they haven't got a tinful of maggots from the tackle shop.

1 February 1968

How sweet is the smell of success?

One of the subjects which anglers are always ready to discuss is the reaction of fish to smells and flavours. The constant recurrence of an advertisement for a substance from America 'guaranteed to produce more and bigger catches, every time', has resulted in a number of readers writing to ask if this, or any other stuff will work.

I can't answer that question directly, because I haven't tried. Perhaps someone who has will write in and share his findings with the rest of us. Meanwhile, I'll tell you what my experience has been with various scents added to baits, either deliberately or accidentally and also what I know about the ability of fish to detect scents and flavours.

Experiments have shown that salmon can detect the smell of the human hand in a most amazing way. They were observed to react shortly after a man, hundreds of yards upstream and concealed completely from the fish, put his hand in the water.

Keen sense

Whether other fish are as well able to detect the human scent, I don't know.

Remember, it is generally believed that salmon are able to distinguish the river in which they were born, and return to it. They achieve this by detecting the subtle difference between what is dissolved in its waters and what is in other rivers, so they may have a far keener sense of smell and taste than other species of fish.

Certainly, other species of fish do have a well developed sense of smell or taste. Some years ago, a tank was established in which several small perch were kept.

When they had settled down and were obviously healthy and thriving, some experiments were made. Right from the start, there was a tube running into the tank, through which a constant stream of water passed, the overflow being carried away via another tube.

The experiments consisted in introducing various flavours via the inflow tube, in such a way that only by sensing these flavours could the perch tell what had been done. They couldn't see the experimenters, or sense the vibration of their movements, or anything of that kind.

Worm flavour

I haven't got all the details of these experiments now, but I do remember that a single drop of water from a container in which some worms had been dipped, set those perch searching energetically around their tank, obviously looking for worms. Not only could they recognise the flavour of worm, but they could do so when the dilution was very high indeed.

A more recent experiment was carried out by Dr. Barrie Rickards, and described in the book *Fishing for Big Pike* which he has recently written in collaboration with Ray Webb. He put down pike traps in drains leading to a Fenland river, several hundred feet from the river itself.

Some traps were baited with herring, some were unbaited. Numbers of pike found their way up these drain and into the baited traps; very few went up the drains or into the traps that were not baited.

Incidentally, Barrie and Ray have definite views about the relative merits of herrings and mackerel as pike dead baits, but if you want to know more about that, buy or borrow their book!

The ability of eels to scent food is almost uncanny. I have followed an eel more than a quarter of a mile up a clear brook, until it found the dead fish it had obviously scented – but I have also watched eels go downstream to a dead bait and how they managed that feat of scenting is more than I can understand, let alone explain.

Salmon roe

I used to have a fair-sized pond in my garden, and I tried various ideas in that, on similar lines to the experiment I've just told you about, with the perch in the tank.

This pond was topped up with water from the mains, via a plastic hose, from time to time to counter losses by evaporation, and I made a gadget that allowed me to introduce flavours into the flow. The favourite with my goldfish, carp and golden orfe was water in which wheat had been boiled.

The solitary tench liked the flavour of oxblood but other species showed no interest in that, None of those fish liked the flavour of fish blood, though such species as pike, perch, trout, zander and chub might have reacted favourably to it, if I'd had any of them in the pond.

One thing that crops up in some of the older angling books is salmon roe, which is held to be a deadly attraction to trout and sea-trout. I believe its use is illegal.

Stoddard, in *The Anglers Companion*, relates how, on 24 November 1837, he used salmon roe paste to send a scent-trail downstream and in about five hours caught 133 trout, including a 5-pounder. On 16 October 1844, he repeated the feat, catching 212 trout, again in about five hours, and he was able to determine that upwards of two-thirds of his catch had travelled upstream for more than 300 yards.

Intrigued by this, I once tried what the potted salmon roe that you can buy in delicatessen shops would do. This stuff is imported from Canada. None of the fish I tried it on was interested; but of course I tried it in the summer, in waters that hold no salmon.

Cheese in mud

There might have been a different story to tell had I tried it in October or November, in a salmon river – including my appearance in a magistrate's court!

Most experienced anglers know that chub can find a bit of cheese-paste in thick, muddy flood water, even after dark, and that the stronger the cheese, the sooner they find it. There seems little doubt, too, that there is a flavour in wasp-grubs that appeals to chub, and at times to other species. I've had some good catches of tench with it.

So there seems no doubt that fish can detect flavours or smells, and are very much attracted by some of them, different species having different preferences. I could never satisfy myself, though, that the scent of a man's hand or of tobacco, had any repellent effect on trout or coarse fish of any species.

Not many anglers wear gloves to mix groundbait or to bait their hooks, and I can't say that when, as an experiment, I've taken elaborate precautions to prevent the scent of my hands from contaminating the bait, I've noticed any increase in my catches.

To sum it up then, some scents attract some kinds of fish, often to a remarkable degree; but they are natural scents, not what the chemists call 'essential oils', things like oil of aniseed, oil of rhodium, oil of spike and the rest.

For most fishing, good ground-baits and hook baits contain their own attractive scents and need no additions. What matters most is where, when and how they are used.

11 November 1971

Rise and fall of deadbait

This week I turn to deadbait fishing for pike as a result of a most interesting letter I had from Mr J. S. Barker, who helps to look after the fish in the Brighton aquarium.

There they have two pike which are fed on sprats. The sprats are usually taken while they are sinking, but Mr Barker has observed that when a sprat reaches the bottom, the pike, as he says moves forward very slowly and when about a foot away, opens its mouth, stretching its gill covers to the fullest extent and then closing its mouth sharply.

'This blows the sprat off the bottom, when it is taken then swallowed. If the pike fails to blow the sprat off the bottom at its first attempt, it repeats the process until the sprat is lifted.'

It isn't always wise to assume that the behaviour of fish in an aquarium or a small garden pond is the same as it would be in a natural river or lake, but in this case, I think it is very likely that pike deal with deadbaits in the same way wherever they happen to be. If so, we had better bear it in mind when we fish deadbaits for pike.

An ordinary dead fish sinks very slowly, if its swim-bladder is punctured. So if we know fairly accurately where a pike is, we should take care that the deadbait does sink slowly, and not load it with lead to make it sink faster. It may be that we had better prevent it from sinking right to the bottom, by using a float set a bit closer to the bait than the depth of the water.

Syringe

I've caught quite a few fair-sized pike on dead fish suspended below a float to keep them off the bottom, not because I thought at the

Dead-baits mounted in this way can often reduce the chances of catching pike. The lower trebles stand a good chance of snagging weed or bottom debris, just as the pike is attempting to blow its intended meal clear of the bottom (Angling Times)

time that this made the baits more attractive to pike, but to keep them from being chewed up by eels.

An alternative would be to use a buoyant deadbait, either one with an intact swim-bladder, or by injecting the dead fish with air from a syringe. That could be fished a little way off the bottom by attaching enough lead to pull it down, a few inches from the bait, a method that would also deal with the problem of bottom weed or soft mud.

When a deadbait sinks, it nearly always reaches bottom with the hooks underneath. If a pike then behaves as Mr Barker describes, it can only blow the fish off the bottom if the fish can move freely. If the hooks catch in weed, or bottom debris, they'll stop the bait from being blown clear. So would any large amount of lead attached to the bait, either inside or out, that might be there to increase casting distance.

In my opinion, a great deal of long casting is done with deadbaits that is a complete waste of effort. The fact that pike are caught by this long casting proves nothing; the pike might have found and taken the same baits only a few yards from the bank, if they'd been fished there.

The fact is that pike can scent a dead fish from a very great distance indeed – a far greater distance than any bait can be cast. It is only when the difference in temperature between deep and shallow water causes pike to swim deep that, on some waters, a long throw is needed to reach the fish. Otherwise, it suffices to toss the bait out just a few yards, which gives you the advantage of a shorter line, with less stretch, on which to hit a pike.

Swallow

Not only that; you can judge better at short range which way the pike is pointing and apply your pull in the opposite direction, by striking to the left, to the right, or straight back, whichever is indicated. At long range, you have no such choice. It makes a difference, believe me, to the number of runs that result in a fish on the bank.

I think it pays when fishing deadbaits to always use a float, because pike will often take such baits and swallow them before moving off. Whether you want to put your pike back or hit them on the head, a swallowed bait is undesirable. A float tells you directly a pike takes and you can tighten at once.

So I always use a float nowadays, and I've noticed that, having set it to cock, the first thing that happens is that it bobs up and lies flat, no doubt because the pike has done exactly what Mr Barker says they do – blown the bait up off the bottom.

By the time I've picked up the rod and taken in any slack, the pike will have grabbed the bait, and I can hit him before he gets it down his throat. That's what happens when the bait is laid on the bottom. But after hearing from Mr Barker, I shall be fishing baits off the bottom, either anchored by a lead on a link, or hung below a float. Which way is best probably depends on conditions.

You can cover a lot of water with a suspended bait, if there is a good breeze or a current, specially if you use a float with plastic vanes to catch the wind when you're fishing lakes. I'm not sure this is always the best method, though; a moving bait is harder for a pike to track down by scent than one that stays in the same place. With two rods, of course, you can try both methods simultaneously.

Or, you can anchor one bait and cast the other well out, pulling it back in a series of small pulls in the direction of the fixed bait, thus laying scent trails that may lead pike to the latter bait sooner, unless one of them takes the bait you're casting instead.

A bait you intend to cast and retrieve needs a bit of lead on a separate wire, attached to the deadbait on the side opposite to the hooks, so the bait can bump the bottom without the hooks catching weed, twigs or sunken leaves. A lead on a separate link isn't good, as it is apt to tangle with the hooks in a long cast.

If your baits are soft and won't stand up to much casting, use a big bar spoon and impale a strip of firm fish on the hooks, so that you lay a scent trail every time you retrieve it. There's a lot to be said for adopting a more active method of fishing with one of your rods, if the weather is cold. It keeps you warmer and it helps to improve your chances.

I am greatly indebted to Mr Barker, who may be able to provide yet more information as a result of his observations.

6 December 1978

Ground rules for baiting

Pre-baiting or baiting-up, and groundbaiting while actually fishing, are of great importance in coarse fishing, but not too well understood by many anglers.

Most people think that baiting-up and groundbaiting are done to attract fish to a particular area. In fact they also serve a much more important purpose . . . that of educating fish to eat what the angler wants them to eat.

No matter how much groundbait you put in, and regardless of how attractive to fish it is, it will seldom attract fish to places where they don't like to be. This depends a good deal on what sort of fish are involved.

Bream, and especially big bream, have their patrol routes and it is nearly impossible to attract the fish away from these. You can, by groundbaiting a place on one of their routes, teach the bream to eat whatever groundbait you decide to use, and you can also hold up the shoal in one place while they mop up your groundbait. But unless you do put the groundbait on their route, it will usually be wasted.

Susceptible

This also applies, though to a lesser extent, to tench. Tench are very susceptible to the amount of light that reaches them. And, if it becomes too bright, they move deeper, to where it is dimmer. Groundbait will therefore only attract them into areas where the light is right. This is a useful thing to know, because it lets you bait-up two or three areas of different depths. You fish the shallowest spot in the dark, or at late evening or early morning. When sport falls of with increasing daylight, you move to your deeper swim, and from there to one deeper still, if that is possible.

Chub can be attracted from considerable distances by groundbaiting, provided their route doesn't take them past something that scares them. From Izaak Walton's time onwards, the chub has been recognised, as he put it, as 'the fearfullest of fishes'. And rightly so. Consequently, if you want to draw chub a long way up stream, you must watch out for the possibility of disturbance between where they start from and where you want them to finish. Generally, it is better to go to the chub rather than try to bring them to you.

I never did find a satisfactory way of groundbaiting for perch. Some of the older fishing books recommend putting half a dozen live minnows in a glass jar, with a mesh cover, and sinking it in the place where you want the perch to come. In a few hours, you are supposed to see dozens of perch round the jar, leering at the minnows inside.

It's never worked for me, probably because wherever there are minnows, a few thousand are swimming around where the perch can get at them; so why should they hang around a jar looking at a few minnows they can't reach?

You can, however, bring perch into a particular area for a little while in several ways. One is by casting a small vibrating spoon out and winding it back, casting in a different direction each time. Another is by what I call indirect groundbaiting, which also works for pike. You use groundbait to attract small fish, which in turn attract the pike or perch. My grandfather always held that the best way to catch pike was to fish for roach, groundbaiting to attract and collect those in one small area, and to have pike tackle ready for when some pike began to attack the roach, either in the swim or those you'd caught and put into a keepnet.

Roach, like chub, can be attracted to where you want them fairly successfully. How successfully depends on conditions of weed and natural food. On very weedy rivers like the Kennet and the Hampshire Avon, with lots of natural food in the weed, it isn't so easy, which is why the roach fishing on these rivers is at its best in autumn and winter, when the weed is considerably less.

Barbel are very peculiar in their feeding habits. In my experience, they are hard to attract into a different area from where they'd otherwise be, and it takes a lot of groundbait to educate them. I should explain that by groundbait, I mean whatever you put in; not just cereal, but maggots, seeds, worms or whatever else you may choose.

Location

With barbel, therefore, it pays to locate the fish if possible and groundbait where they are. In Victorian times it was not unusual for anglers to pay a Thames professional fisherman to bait-up barbel swims with 5,000 to 10,000 lobworms, which sometimes resulted in catches exceeding a hundredweight, and sometimes one small eel. I suspect that the failures were usually due to a wrong choice of swim, rather than a reluctance on the part of the barbel to eat worms.

Carp are apt to roam extensively about a lake, though it is obviously good sense to bait-up areas where you see signs of their feeding. I had a lesson from Kevin Clifford in how effective a catapult for shooting seed baits can be in carp fishing, on the same occasion when he, perhaps, learned a bit about the effectiveness of bright betalight floats.

I cast out the float tackle and he bombarded the float with sweet corn. It was not very long before some carp were successfully landed.

This method avoids the annoyance of finding, after baiting up for days, that some other angler has appropriated the pitch you had intended to fish. Scatter your corn, beans or whatever it is, far and wide, to educate the carp. When you come to fish, choice of pitch isn't so desperately important because you can use a few pouchfulls of seed to bring some of the carp to you.

Incidentally, I find myself using floats more and more for carp fishing, now we have these bright betalights for night work. There's a limit, in practice about 30-35 yards, to the range at which you can use them. But on the lakes I fish that is more than enough.

You don't need much groundbait to attract eels.

They'll scent a single dead fish from very great distances and home on to it, as they will on almost anything eatable. If you want plenty in one spot, tie a dead trout, pierced all over with a knife or skewer, on a bit of string and chuck it out.

If eels are in the water, they'll be around that trout, trying to eat it, in half an hour. You can then pull it out and replace it with a small fish, a piece of fish or fish guts, or a worm, on hook. You may attract pike or zander as well.

20 June 1979

Grain of truth

My goodness, it has taken enough time for anglers generally, and specially match anglers, to get around to thinking about sweet-corn.

I was looking up some articles I wrote in the early years of *Angling Times* the other day, and I came across one written before 1956, in which I mentioned that maize, properly stewed, was a very useful bait.

Sweetcorn is, of course, nothing but maize cut before the grains have become hard. They've been using it for bait in the USA for a century or more, to considerable effect. Over there, they simply soak hard maize, which does very little to soften it, and chuck it in as groundbait.

The fact that after a time, the wet maize ferments and stinks horribly, doesn't seem to put the fish off it at all. The hookbait is, of course, a soft grain or two.

But there's no difficulty in making hard maize soft; you simply cook it in a pressure cooker at top pressure, 14lb per square inch,

A handful of sweetcorn, a superb and economical bait for many species of fish (Angling Times)

for about an hour. If you think the sweet flavour of the tinned stuff matters, just add treacle.

I've done a great deal of fishing with maize, so perhaps a few facts may help any anglers who are thinking of trying it for the first time, and specially matchmen.

First of all, it is not a small fish bait. Minnows and bleak simply can't get it into their mouths, and it takes a very big gudgeon to do so. I've never caught a roach or bream under half a pound on it. So any matchman who draws a peg at which his only chance is to scratch for tiddlers had better keep off fishing with whole maize.

83

Economical

Second, it is fairly heavy and sinks much more quickly than maggots or casters. Unless it is chopped up, it will go down through the bleak and other small fish to the better stuff on or near the bottom.

Third, it is economical. It doesn't take much to get fish feeding on it, nor does it take long.

Fourth, it lets you use a fairly strong line and a good sized hook – size 12 for a single grain, but you can go as big as size 10 where there are bigger fish. You don't want to go smaller than a 12, or the hook is likely to be guarded by the bait and fail to penetrate.

I doubt if the colour of the hook makes any difference, but maize looks best on gilt hooks. Because it is fairly heavy, you don't need a fine line to let it behave naturally in a current. I usually fish single grains, for roach and bream, on 3lb line; two or three grains on a size 8 for tench four or five on a size 4 for carp, chub or barbel.

There aren't hard-and-fast rules, but if you get big fish feeding on maize, you'll usually find them willing to take several grains at once, all on a hook, and that lets you use a bigger and stronger hook.

Accurately

Fifth, maize is a good bait for fishing at long range. Not only does it stay on the hook in a long cast; it can also be shot much farther with a catapult than can maggots, casters or small seeds. And more accurately.

Sixth, it is filling stuff. You can easily over-feed with it, specially with species like roach and bream. It's easy for the fish to mop up, though, so it won't hold a shoal of bream so long as will cereal ground baits, or squatts, or worms in mud balls.

For bigger species like carp, barbel and the better class chub, you can compensate for the speed at which fish eat it by putting more in; a double-figure barbel or carp can eat half a pint and still be keen for more, and a big chub will chomp nearly as much. But go easy with it for roach and bream.

Seventh, where a good deal has been put into a limited area, fish will pick up the bait and then mop up the loose stuff without moving far. This may lead to bites being undetected, or thought to be not positive enough to strike, when in fact the bait has not only been taken but swallowed. That usually leads to the nylon being bitten through by the throat teeth of the fish; when you recover the tackle, the hook is missing. That can happen with carp, barbel and chub.

So it becomes very necessary to use a sensitive means of detecting bites, and to strike at the slightest indication. This is so important that for fishing with maize, I nearly always use float tackle where circumstances allow it, even for carp; and when fishing still waters or slacks in rivers, I have the shot as near the hook as the size of the fish allows.

Obviously, you can hardly put the shot an inch from the hook when you're after double-figure carp, or you'll strike all too often at false bites. In that case, I'd put the shot about 9 inches from the hook and set the float at from two to three times the depth, so as to have a small angle between the line and the bottom.

Whether legering, float-fishing or laying on, it's sensible to keep the distance between lead and hook as short as the size of the fish you're seeking will allow.

Eighth, because maize sinks fast, most of what you throw or shoot in will end up on the bottom; not a lot gets intercepted while it is sinking. Where I've been able to watch it sink among fish, I've noticed that nearly all the fish wait till it reaches the bottom and pick it up from there, rather than try to take it as it sinks. For that reason it is most effective when fished in a way that lets the baited hook lie still on the bottom.

It doesn't catch nearly so many fish when worked on the drop, or trotted down the current under a float, either off bottom or dragging.

Ninth, maize – or sweetcorn – is a conspicuous colour. Fish can see it more easily in muddy or coloured water than they can most other baits, and it shows up well on the bottom. Since it also has a distinctive scent or flavour, it is easy for fish to find in any conditions of water and light.

All-round

It is not, as many anglers seem to think, a bait only for carp, or only a specimen hunter's bait. It's a very good, clean, all-round bait and if you pressure-cook maize instead of buying canned sweetcorn, it's very cheap too.

If it fails to catch you fish on almost any sort of coarse fish water, either you chose a bad day when fish were simply not feeding, or your method of fishing it was wrong.

3 July 1981

Give 'em a pasting!

When I was a boy, bread paste was by far the most popular and widely-used coarse-fish bait in southern England.

Tackle shops didn't sell maggots in those days, or worms either. The only bait they did sell was cornflour, flavoured with aniseed which came in a match-box type packing smaller than a packet of ten cigarettes.

It was called 'King's Natural Bait', and was a very expensive way of buying cornflour with aniseed flavouring – rather like 'Silver Cloud' ground bait, which was a very expensive way of buying sand mixed with the waste from a dog-biscuit factory.

Combination

So, we youngsters made our own bread paste, and used the waste crusts, soaked and pounded up with bran, for groundbait. We caught plenty of good fish with this combination.

Not very long ago, I wrote about bait additives and colourings in *Angling Times*, and to my surprise, I received quite a lot of enquiries about how to make the basic paste to which scents, colourings and other materials can be added.

Evidently there are very many anglers who don't know how to make bread paste. In fact, we seem to have reached a stage where half our coarse-fish anglers would give up fishing if they couldn't buy maggots or casters from a shop.

Which seems to me to be a great pity, because although big fish can be and are caught on maggots, there are many better baits to use if you want quality fish rather than tiddlers. Bread paste is one of them – one of the best, even without colouring or extra flavours. If you check the record list, you'll find that hardly any of the record fish were caught on maggots or casters.

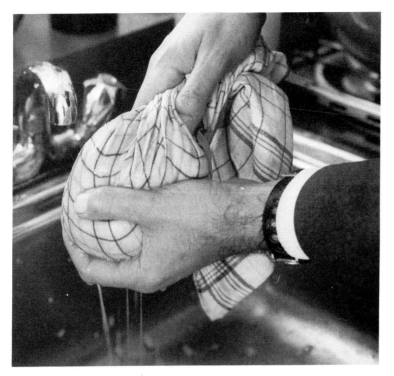

The correct way to make paste – clean hands, clean cloth and clean water. Squeezing and kneading will produce a putty-like consistency that makes a perfect bait for all fish (Angling Times)

By the time readers of long experience have read this far, they'll probably be saying 'Surely, everyone knows how to make bread paste!' I hope they'll forgive me for saying that half our coarse-fish anglers don't and also for explaining how it is done.

You need a loaf, at least one full day old. New bread won't do, and very stale loaves make the job more difficult. Cut off all the crust. You can bake it in an oven and pound it into dry crumbs for making ground bait, or soak it and mash it up as it is, or you may like to save some of it to cut into cubes for hook bait.

Cut the crumb into slices about an inch thick and dip them in clean water. Make sure your hands are clean too. Then put all the wet bread into a cloth, such as a kitchen towel or a piece of linen, bring the edges of the cloth together and twist them. The bread will form a ball inside the cloth – keep twisting and squeezing the ball, till you've pressed out as much water as possible.

Texture

Now take the bread out of the cloth and knead it in your hands till it's soft like putty. Pat or roll it out flat, fold it, knead it again, and repeat this till you have a uniform texture throughout the ball.

If it seems too soft, you can stiffen it by adding some plain, not self-raising-flour. But don't make it too stiff. Fish like it soft. That fine angler Peter Stone uses very soft paste. I remember Fred J. Taylor once saying: 'Stoney, the fish don't eat your paste – they drink it!'

True, with soft paste, you'll have to put on a fresh bait for every cast, but the lost bits are acting as ground bait and you'll catch more fish with the soft stuff – not only because fish prefer it but also because it doesn't interfere with hook penetration when you tighten on a bite.

Some of the older fishing books recommended adding cotton wool to bread paste so that it stayed on the hook for cast after cast. Don't do it!

You can make bread paste with white or brown bread. As boys we always used white, but it is worth remembering that two record carp were caught with brown, flavoured with honey – Albert Buckley's 26-pounder from Mapperley and Bob Richard's 31¼ pounder from Redmire Pool.

Bread paste also provides a base to which you can add other ingredients or colours. Some of the enzymes, amino acids, proteins and other additives favoured by carp fishers may help, but most anglers will favour simpler things like cheese.

Atmosphere

It's worth considering how to make good cheese paste. First, you make your bread paste. Then you take some cheese that has been left in a warm atmosphere for long enough, and knead it into a smooth paste. If there is any hardened outside, cut it off before kneading. Then pat or roll both the bread paste and the cheese flat, on a board. Lay one on top of the other. Pat or roll, fold, pat or roll again, fold, and keep on folding and flattening till both cheese and paste are well and truly mixed. Above all, keep it very soft – add water if necessary.

GLING CLUB

HOTEL, SHREWSBURY

ELLICOE-WALL

—

GE

se

rtage

RY

MATCH SECRETARY
D. WILLIAMS
71 North Street
Castlefields
SHREWSBURY
Tel: 64693

RICHARDSON
LOW, Esq.

in Cheque for £3 = 00 Ano

s your Membership Cards Ano

room for your information Mr/R

if you or your Friends

it is not Advisable to phone

4506

Yours faithfully

J. rivorde se.

Reference our out Kania
Coast Carriers.

McHardys of Carlisle

Fishing Tackle Specialists   South Henry Street, Carlisle, Cumbria, England.   Telephone: Carlisle 23988

We thank you for your valued order. The balance of
the new items will follow as soon as possible.

Items to follow

Balance as recent.

Dear Mr Talbot

Thank you for
I have pleasure in enclo
Car stickers.

I have also
For locating the water
Have any problems
Me on Shrewsbury

Hardens

Cheese paste hardens in water, and the colder the water, the more it hardens. Remember, you'll have to strike the hook out of the paste and into a biting fish and if the paste is too hard, you won't do it.

All sorts of other things can be added to bread paste, such as tinned pet food, soaked and crushed trout pellets, egg yolk, honey and literally hundreds of other substances. But whatever you use, the principle is the same – put the additive on flattened bread paste, fold, flatten, fold again, flatten again and keep on doing this until you have a perfect mix.

Sounds as if it takes ages, doesn't it? In fact, it may take as long as a full ten minutes, and it's well worth the very little time and trouble that it takes.

Remember that it all depends on making a good sample of bread paste right at the start, which ever additives you may choose.

Deep-freeze

When you've completed your paste mix, roll it into a ball, enclose it in a damp cloth and put it into an unventilated box or tin. If you're not going to use it at once, keep it in a fridge, and if you make up big quantities, which is not a bad idea, you can deep-freeze it.

Keep an eye on any you have in use because it can go sour and put fish off, especially in warm weather. Sniff it! You'll soon know if it has 'gone off'.

There you are then. If you didn't know before, you know how to make bread paste now – and I repeat, it'll catch you more big fish of most sorts than maggots or casters ever will.

28 April 1982

PART III
TACTICS AND SKILLS

If you keep on missing bites – slack off

Many of the letters I receive from readers ask for advice about missed bites on leger tackle. What happens is that they get solid pulls which, no matter what they try, they cannot convert into hooked fish. It usually turns out that they are fishing downstream at comparatively short range.

The natural reaction of most anglers to missed bites is to strike faster and faster; so, because fast striking is difficult on a slack line, the tendency is to keep the line as tight as possible between rod-tip and lead, and hammer every pull as quickly as possible.

Fish feel resistance

If this is persisted in, the angler may eventually hit one or two of the fish, though he still misses most of them. He goes away babbling about the lightning speed needed to hit these bites.

What is happening is that the fish are feeling the resistance of the rod-top directly they bite. Nine times out of ten, they eject the bait before the angler can strike. The tighter he keeps his line while awaiting a bite, the more easily the fish can feel the rod.

There are several ways in which the problem can be tackled. Here they are:

(1) Assuming you're right-handed, hold the line between butt ring and reel in your left hand, with a couple of feet of loose line between hand and reel. Point the rod straight at the lead, and let go the line directly you feel the least touch. Then strike. If you still miss, try increasing the loose line.

(2) After casting and allowing the lead to settle, deliberately pay off some slack line instead of drawing up tight. Strike in the usual way.

(3) Try a dough-bobbin, just heavy enough to counteract the pull of the current on the line. Keep the rod pointed at the lead to avoid ring-friction.

(4) Fish the swim from below instead of above, ie leger upstream with only just enough lead to hold, and watch for slackline bites.

(5) If the current and general nature of the swim allow it, use a float, either in the water or in the air. No, I'm not crazy. A fairly

heavy float can be used to act like a dough-bobbin in that position when you're using a static leger at fairly long range; but you don't usually get these hard-to-hit bites then.

Avoid direct pull on tip

You see what all this is aimed at, don't you? That's right, avoiding a direct pull on the rod tip when a fish bites.

You may devise other ways perhaps even better than those I've listed. What you mustn't do is to tighten up and crouch like a cobra about to strike, in an attempt to match your striking speed against the spitting-out speed of the fish. If you do, you will seldom win.

All this, of course, assumes that your lead has been correctly chosen and isn't too heavy for the swim you are fishing. The general tendency among anglers is to use far too much lead. I've seen people using 1oz bombs in swims where a couple of swan shot would have been plenty.

Bites from small fish

I am also assuming that the missed bites are from fish that one could reasonably hope to catch on the tackle in use. When I'm fishing for barbel with a size 4 hook on a 9lb line, I get plenty of knocks from dace and gudgeon, some of which jerk the rod-top down 3 or 4 inches.

I don't expect to hit such bites. I don't even try. The small fish that produce them could hardly get the bait into their mouths; if they did succeed, the indication would be even more positive than it is.

By using different end tackle, I could catch these little fish, especially if I took steps to prevent them from feeling the resistance of the rod. But I don't want to catch them. I'd sooner they did feel the resistance. It makes them let go.

If a barbel takes the bait I shan't miss him! He'll either give a really solid pull and almost hook himself, or I shall feel that characteristic trembling barbel bite against which the rod-top offers no resistance anyway because the fish isn't pulling.

You must change your method

Chub and roach are the difficult species, especially roach, which are very sensitive to resistance of any kind when you are legering.

The main thing to remember is that if you keep missing bites and you are reasonably sure that they're coming from the fish you are trying to catch, you must do something about it. It's no good keeping on with the same method because you'll only keep on missing.

How can you be sure what fish are producing the bites? You can't always. If you suspect small fish, you can always try a much smaller hook and bait. If that produces small fish, you'll have learned the kind of bite they give and ignore it when you revert to the bigger hook and bait.

11 September 1964

To try a swollen river is always a gamble

So many readers have written to ask for advice about fishing in conditions of high water or floods, that this week I'm going to answer here, instead of by individual letters.

But before talking about flood fishing, here's a bit of advice. If you know of a good lake, fish it in preference to a flooded river unless you're the sort of person who likes to back outsiders.

Fishing flooded rivers is chancy. Now and then you'll strike lucky and make a tremendous catch, or land an extra-big fish. Much more often you'll have little or nothing to show for a day's fishing in floodwater.

Even if you follow the advice that most experienced anglers would give you about fishing floods, you'll often find fish few and far between.

I'll give you an example. Not long ago a match was fished on the Ouse at Offord. The river there holds plenty of good fish. In recent years, a large rectangular pool has been excavated alongside the river, to form a Marina with moorings for cabin cruisers and other craft with a channel joining the river.

I was wrong
Some very good fish have been caught from the still waters of this

pool when the river was normal, and when I heard that it was included in the area pegged for the match, which was fished in the rain with the main river bank-high and coloured, I'd have laid any sum on big weights coming from some of the pegs round the pool.

I should have expected hordes of big fish to have moved into it to avoid the heavy water and muck in the main river.

As it turned out, catches were extremely poor. Fish don't always behave according to the book!

Nevertheless, one of the first principles of flood water fishing is to find a place where the current is moderate and the bottom is clean; and if the water in it is less filthy than that of the main current, so much the better.

Often a feeder stream is carrying clearer water and forming a slow eddy where it joins the river; such places are always worth a trial.

Drainage ditches that are insignificant when a river is at normal level are often backed up to a depth of several feet when the river is bank-high. Such places often hold fish, sometimes lots of big fish. So do worn-down places in the banks where cattle are in the habit of coming down to drink.

Some rivers have a sort of stepped formation of bank; reeds or sedges fringe the margin at normal level, then there is a bit of flat bank with a higher bank behind.

This flat piece is often covered with short grass cropped by cattle or sheep. When the river rises and covers it, fish move on to it. probably attracted by the insects and worms they can find there.

It can often be located easily, because you can still see the reeds that mark the proper margin projecting above the surface. Even when the water between these and the steeper part of the bank is only a foot deep, fish will usually be there. Sometimes you can even see the swirls they make.

I need hardly tell you that if you can find places of this kind, your chances of catching fish are excellent. Remember that the fish in them are looking for such things as worms, slugs, and leather-jackets, and choose your hook-baits accordingly.

Careful watch
Remember too that such places can be treacherous and choose tackle accordingly. Hook a big bream, chub or barbel, and he will

very likely crash straight through that marginal growth of reeds, rushes, grass, dead willow herb and nettle-stalks.

A line of 5lb bs or more may hold; one of lesser strength probably won't.

Movements of fish into flooded grassy areas isn't confined to these narrow pieces of course. Some rivers wander through flat water-meadows and when these are well flooded, fish may be almost anywhere.

A careful watch may reveal their whereabouts, however. You may see a fish swirl or turn over at the surface, or, if the surface is calm, it is sometimes possible to detect a place where mud is being stirred up by a shoal.

I've had more than one good catch of fish where a narrow lane ran down to a ford across a small river. When the floods were up, two beautiful slacks formed, one on each side of the river, where that lane was. These slacks had gravel bottoms, of course, and they held plenty of fish.

For some odd reason, the roach were always on one side, while the other held perch, dace and chub of various sizes.

Talking of Offord earlier in this article, reminds me of a ditch there that runs into a sidestream. A sort of bridge crosses this ditch, level with the ground.

More than once I've caught good chub under that bridge when the river had been in flood, though it is 60 or 70 yards from the river. In floods, any sort of sidestream, ditch or carrier may hold fish if its current is appreciably less than the main river.

Don't forget, though, that even when a river is roaring down there can be slow currents below fast surface water. Whenever the depth is much greater than average, such places are liable to be found; and one of them is below a weir.

Whether you can get into a position that allows you to work a bait under the sill depends upon the surroundings; often this is impossible, but when it is possible, it is well worth trying.

It's a thought

I often think, when I'm sitting fishing a river that is tearing by in full flood, taking millions of gallons of water away into the sea every hour, that within a few months the Water Authorities will be busy abstracting those same rivers to mere trickles, while the River Authorities are busy with their excavators and draglines making sure no water stays on the land next time it rains.

11 March 1966

Exploding some legering myths

One of the problems which exercises anglers' minds is how to per-suade leger tackle to hold its position in fast water. Let's have a look at the factors involved.

Consider the simplest kind of running leger, where the line is threaded through a hole in a ball of lead, and prevented from slid-ing down to the hook by a stop-shot. Here we have the pressure of the current on the line above the lead, on the lead itself, on the stop-shot, on the line below the stop-shot and on the baited hook.

As Alan Barker pointed out in an article in *Fishing* magazine, it's the current pressure on the line above the lead that causes the lead to shift. By itself, the lead would stay put, at least temporarily, in most swims, especially as once it has reached the bottom, it is out of the fastest water. The current is always fastest near the surface, and the line to the lead has to pass through faster water than the water where the lead is lying.

A good deal of confusion has arisen from considering the move-ment of leads by the current, irrespective of the pull in the line. When stones are moved by currents, an eddy forms behind the stone which has an undercutting effect, eventually washing away some of the bottom silt or sand just downstream of the stone. The stone then slides down into the depression or the current gets under it and lifts it downstream a bit. The process is then repeated, with variations as the river changes from a spate to a trickle and so on.

Eliminate eddy
Because of this well-known effect, people incline towards stream-lined leads, which are supposed to eliminate the eddy or tur-bulence downstream of the lead. Always supposing that this

97

turbulence can actually be eliminated, it doesn't matter whether the lead has a flat surface in contact with the bottom or not, a point worth thinking about.

In any case, this effect of the turbulence washing away part of the bottom, always supposing that it is the kind of bottom that can be washed away, and not solid rock, takes time. It isn't this effect which causes your lead to fail to hold bottom.

The shape of lead hardest to shift is the one that has maximum weight for its frontal area, and which requires the greatest amount of force to turn it over. A long, thin lead with the line attached to one end will hold better than a spherical one.

What is much more important than trying to improve the holding qualities of the lead, is reducing the pull on the lead by reducing the drag in the line. This depends not only on the length of line under water but also on the speed of the current through which it passes. Of course the current speed isn't constant over the whole of the submerged line, nor is the set-up constant for every swim.

Deciding how the rod-tip shall be placed relative to the lead after casting out is part of the leger-fisher's art. He has to size up the problem in the swim he is fishing, and set his rod, or hold it, so as to keep current pressure on his line to a minimum. Obviously, if he is casting well beyond a fast middle current, he will want to keep his rod-top high, and a long rod will be a great help. His line can then be made to miss the middle current.

If on the other hand he wants his lead plumb in the middle of the fast water, he may find a low rod-top position more successful to make his line pass under the faster surface water.

The thinner the line, the less the pressure of the water on it, but the difficulty here is that one usually needs a strongish line to deal with big fish in fast water. Clearly, the thinner the line is for a given strength, the less lead will be needed to hold bottom. The modern super-strength lines can help, but it is well to remember that these lines have less stretch and break more easily on the strike. Legering in fast water often produces savage bites, and some self-discipline is needed to avoid responding with a savage strike. Here, a change to a more flexible rod can help minimise the danger of breakage.

Balance forces

It is a common fallacy that in fast water legering, a biting fish pulls line through the swivel of the lead, or through the hole in a bored lead, or the nylon loop of a string of swan shot. What happens, invariably, is that the lead is moved, and if the lead is well chosen, the fish feels very little resistance in the process. The reason is that the various forces produced by the current are nearly enough to move the lead, so that only a tiny pull from the fish is needed to move it.

That being the case, you're not losing anything by increasing the size of the lead to hold bottom. It's all a matter of balancing the forces; and that isn't just a matter of choosing a lead that will just, and only just, hold bottom. You still have a measure of control after you have cast out. After the lead has settled, you can tighten up to a point just short of what will shift the lead. This is part of the art of touch legering; to feel your lead on the bottom and tension your line to the point where the tiniest increase would cause the lead to shift.

This is at its peak in upstream legering, and it should never be forgotten that it is often possible to solve a holding problem by legering upstream instead of down. I find a great deal of reluctance on the part of anglers generally to try this, probably arising from the fact that to do it properly, it is necessary to hold the rod and not put it in a rest.

You have to keep in sensitive contact with your lead all the time, and school yourself to strike when you cease to feel the lead. The great majority of bites are indicated by the line going slack and a long, sweeping strike is needed to connect with the fish.

Here again, great care is needed to avoid breakage when the super-strong type of nylon is used.

It is worth remembering that in swims of moderate flow, upstream float-legering is also possible and can sometimes be very effective. If you achieve a nice balance between the lead and the pull of the current on the line and float above it, you can rest your rod and watch for the float to lift and come back downstream towards you.

I wonder how many anglers are keen enough to go out and experiment with the balance and holding qualities of various tackles, with no bait or hook in the coarse-fish close season?

2 May 1968

That vital link from float to tip-ring

When anglers talk about float-fishing, they'll discuss different kinds of float, different systems of shotting, and a whole lot of other things; but you hardly ever hear them talking about the line between the float and the tip-ring.

Yet it is the control and use of this piece of line that often distinguishes the expert from the novice; that may decide between making a good catch or a blank.

Suppose you're fishing a lake or pond. You will usually find there is some surface drift, even if there isn't any wind. This surface drift acts on the line lying on the water between the float and the rod tip. If you allow it to do so, it will drag your float along. If you want to avoid that, you must keep lifting the line, without moving the float, and laying it back on the water where it came from. Your float and shotting must be heavy enough to allow you to do this without pulling the float towards you.

Or you can sink the line between the rod and the float, out of the way of wind or surface drift, preferably attaching the float by its bottom end only. That will impede your strike somewhat, but in many cases it remains the best thing to do.

But you may not want your float and tackle to stay in one place. It may be better to allow wind or drift to act on the line so as to pull the tackle along. If the drift or the wind is in the right direction, you can use it to cover quite a large area. Many kinds of fish will readily take a moving or dragging bait.

The late Wilfred Cutting who once held the roach record, used to catch large numbers of big perch from Hornsea Mere by using the wind acting on his line to drag a bait along. I have used this method many times to catch rudd, roach and perch, and sometimes it can be very effective for tench.

In running water, there are infinite possibilities for line-control. If you are fishing in an upstream wind, you can keep your line high, let the wind act on it, and so slow down the speed at which your float goes downstream. If the wind is enough you can sometimes use it to stop the float altogether without it swinging nearer to the bank from which you are fishing.

If you want the float to go faster, you keep the rod-point low and let more line lie on the surface.

With the wind coming from behind you, you can use its effect on the line to move your float farther out across the current as it travels.

Crafty trick

With a downstream wind, even without any wind at all, you can sometimes work a very crafty trick, especially if you are casting beyond the fastest part of the current. What you do is to let a bow of line form downstream of your float – running ahead of the float, in fact. Then lower your rod-point and pull. This will pull on the float and cause your bait to rise a little.

A rising bait, especially when it's a maggot, caster or small worm, is very attractive to all kinds of fish. Note that this is a different effect from what you do when you hold the float back. That makes the bait rise too, but gives it the appearance of being able to swim up against the current.

Pulling on a downstream loop makes it rise, but rise with the current, which is what all kinds of nymphs do when they decide it's time to come up and hatch into flies. Your maggot or caster may not resemble these nymphs but at least it's doing what the fish often see their natural food do, and the movement does provoke a lot of bites. You have to be very alert because often the bite comes directly you start the draw.

It takes practice to master these various tricks of line-control, and you sometimes find that making changes, not only in the size and shape of float and its shotting, but also in the size and kind of line you use, can help. For example, when you want to have as much wind-pressure on your line as possible, a braided nylon or terylene line is better than nylon monofil.

If you want to keep your line out of the way of wind, on the other hand, then never use a braided line, which has much more air and water resistance than a monofil one.

Sometimes it's a job to get monofil line to sink. If your float is attached bottom-end only, you can put your rod-tip under water and tighten the line till it pulls under water, but with very light float tackle that often results in the tackle being pulled out of position. There are also conditions in which poking a rod-tip into the water could scare fish.

In fly-fishing, it is often necessary to arrange for the nylon leader to float, or sink, or to be partly sunk and partly on the surface, and to that end I carry not only a tin of silicone line grease but also a little plastic container in which there is a ball of what might be called synthetic detergent mud. You can make this by mixing Fullers earth – which you can buy through a chemist – with any washing-up liquid. Mix it so that it is about the same consistency as plasticene.

Pike fishing

Not only is it useful for fly-fishing; it is also very handy for making monofil sink in any kind of fishing, so it goes with me whether I'm going fly-fishing, float-fishing or legering. All that is necessary is to draw the nylon through the mud-ball. It can make all the difference when you're float-fishing, and sometimes even when you're legering at long range and casting across a stiff breeze. The line will sink directly you get it down on the water.

One special kind of float-fishing where the line above the float is extra important is pike-fishing with a live or dead fish for bait. The line usually has to be a strong one, not only to deal with the possibility of hooking an extra large fish, but also to set the hooks into a very hard, bony mouth. But if this strong line sinks, it's difficult to strike properly; and if you want a livebait to travel, you won't succeed if it has the drag of a sunken line on it.

Fly lines

I find the new soft monofils float better than other monofils if they're lightly greased with a silicone line-grease; but Fred Buller is now using floating level fly lines, the bubble type, which he has been able to get from the USA in 100 yard lengths.

An alternative might be the Mallard floating line, if 100 yard lengths could be obtained. Braided terylene, even if greased well, doesn't stay on the surface long in the strengths we need for pike-fishing, though it's quite all right for long-trotting in the finer sizes.

Yes, there's no doubt about it, choosing the right kind of line and learning to control it makes a tremendous difference to your float-fishing catches.

15 January 1970

Tactics for the new season's early days

Only a few weeks to go before the coarse fishing season starts – which poses the usual problem of which species to go after and where to go.

I suppose most anglers think of carp and tench as species for early season fishing, despite, the fact that they're often still spawning on or after 16 June. I think that this will certainly be so this year; but even if it is, not every carp, nor every tench, spawns every year. It's been proved that carp in some waters spawn only every third or fourth year, so in such waters, only one third or one quarter of the fish will be spawning.

That means fishing well away from the spawning areas, which aren't difficult to locate.

It's odd, isn't it, that pike, which are the first to spawn of all coarse fish, and the quickest to regain condition after spawning, may not be fished for until October in many areas!

Next to spawn after the pike are perch and they, too, regain condition very quickly. In fact they seem to stand up to the effort of spawning much better than other species and are usually pretty fit when the fishing season starts. The only trouble is that they're hard to find and hard to catch, at any rate where the big ones are concerned, until September, especially in rivers. The shoals that assemble to spawn break up and the fish are dotted about in ones and twos all along the river.

Impossible

Thirty years ago, when there were far, far fewer anglers than there are to-day, you could wander along the bank, dropping a bait into likely places, and pick up a fish here, another there, and so on. That's impossible on most fisheries now, so perch fishing in summer is dubious.

On large lakes and reservoirs the perch don't seem to spread out so much and if you can locate them, you can enjoy excellent sport, fishing in one spot.

Chub have always seemed to me to be very variable from the point of view of the effect on them of spawning. Maybe like carp, individual fish don't spawn every year. You find that some you catch are quite fit and strong while others are spiritless and flabby. Still, you can treat them kindly and release them as you catch them, instead of keeping them for hours in nets, so there's no harm in fishing for them as soon as the season opens.

Much the same applies to bream. You may find them in poor condition in June, specially those that live in still waters, but if you use a bit of commonsense, catching them won't harm them. I prefer not to take them from the landing net, or even lift them from the water. If you raise the net enough to prevent the fish splashing about, you can get the hook out with a pair of artery forceps and then lower the net again so as to let the fish swim away. That way the bream is uninjured and you don't get slime all over your hands.

The only time I lift bream right out is when I want to weigh or photograph an exceptional specimen. Fish take no harm from being laid for a few seconds on a patch of long, soft grass that has been well drenched with three of four buckets of water.

Roach fishing in June is another variable business. I've known seasons when the roach were pathetic, thoroughly out of condition and no pleasure at all to catch. In other seasons they've been quite clean, bright and fit on opening day. In these last few years, roach stocks have diminished seriously and I'd have to be convinced that the roach were in really good order before I fished for them in June this year.

Dace, on the other hand, are nearly always all right and if you want to see what you can do with them and a fly rod, the beginning of the season is the best time to try, before the weeds get too thick. The very biggest dace can be caught that way. If someone bet me a large sum that I couldn't catch a pound dace, I'd make fly-fishing my first choice of method in trying to win it.

I've never caught either rudd or barbel in the first weeks of the season that seemed to me to be still out of condition after spawning. Rudd, of course, are absolute suckers for artificial flies and it's a lovely way to catch them.

As with dace, the method is no handicap to catching really big ones, specially in summer, but really, you can catch rudd in almost any way you fancy. In many waters, you can even catch them by spinning; I like to use a tiny gold fly-spoon, cast from a fixed spool reel with a couple of swan-shot ahead of it. Or you can try a white

Polystickle, size 12, fished the same way.

Barbel, of course, are also fish that don't mind chomping another fish, specially in June and a dead minnow, or better still, a dead loach, fished right on the bottom, can sometimes be deadly. Don't be surprised if it also catches chub, perch, eels and trout, if there are any in the barbel swim you choose.

Effective

A small dead fish is a very natural bait and that reminds me that early in the season, natural baits often score over unnatural ones. Coarse fish don't see much in the way of bread, cheese or maggots in the close season. Consequently, in the first week or two after 16 June, baits like crayfish, dead fish, lobworms and lamprey larvae can often be spectacularly effective.

Pre-baiting is always a good idea, not only to attract fish but because it takes you to the waterside before the season begins, and then you discover a lot that helps you to make a good catch. I can't think why so many anglers stay away from the water till 16 June. Advance reconnaissance pays and pays handsomely, believe me!

21 May 1970

Rushes

When I'm river fishing in the winter, what I like to find is a nice bed of rushes. I'm using the term to include all sorts of similar growths, such as reeds, flags and sedges, but the ones I like best are those with dark green, round section leaves.

These are the true rushes, the sort that were used to make rushlights before candles were invented. Our ancestors thought more of them than we do; they used them for lights, for floor coverings and for thatch, and they wove them into baskets.

The reason I like them is that they help my fishing. If there's a bed of them lining the bank from which I'm fishing, and I can find a suitable spot upstream, from which I can trot down, or stretpeg, alongside the rushes, I expect to catch some fish.

A perfect stretch of small river for the lone angler. A combination of rushes, reeds and bankside cover provide all kinds of collecting places for food, and fish

Shelter

What's more, nobody else can move in 15 or 20 yards downstream and spoil my chances.

I know that there will be fish sheltering along the stems, even when those stems are brown and dead, specially if the river is running high and fast.

Rush beds are also found out in mid-stream in shallow rivers and even when they have been reduced by the frosts to nothing more than short, dark brown stubs, they still slow down the current and produce a pocket of slower water at the downstream end of the bed.

This is a place where food, and consequently fish, are liable to collect and where one can fish with comparatively light laying-on tackle, so that very delicate bites can be detected.

In cold weather, you may often need to use very small baits to attract bites, and if you succeed, the bites will be very small touches that need lightly-loaded tackle to register. The downstream end of a rush bed is a good place to try in such conditions.

If it doesn't harbour roach, dace, bream or chub, there's a good chance that either a pike or a few good perch are there instead.

Then there's the rush bed on the opposite bank. If the river isn't too wide, it's always a good idea to run a float tackle along the edge of such a bed, specially if it is good and wide, so that not only can it harbour plenty of fish, but it also prevents other people, on the other bank, from disturbing them.

There used to be a time when you could anchor a boat on the bigger rivers, and trot down alongside rush or reed beds, but nowadays you're liable to be run down by cabin-cruiser cowboys if you try it.

Not long ago, I explained how Ken Taylor fishes close up to rush beds lining the opposite bank, when he is after big perch, by using a peacock quill float threaded on his line from end to end, with a swan shot close up against its bottom end. This has the double advantage of passing through rushes without catching, and of travelling ahead of the bait, so that you can cast to hit the outer rush stems.

I think it is wise always to arrange the tackle so that it can go through the rushes, if you're fishing close up to them, if you don't want to thread your line through a peacock quill, you can use two bits of valve rubber for end caps.

Better still, use those shaped cycle valve rubbers, one at each end. It also pays to use a string of little shots rather than fewer, bigger ones.

If you put the shots all touching one another, they'll go through weed or rushes much more easily. So will those neat little French 'Crottes de Souris' leads – mouse droppings, it means.

They cost more than split shot, but wherever there's rush or weed to contend with, they're worth the extra money.

Rush beds sometimes let you play a useful little trick, that of anchoring float tackle by casting so that your line is caught on a rush stem, or rather, lying over one. This comes in handy when you're casting across a current strong enough to shift your tackle out of position.

It lets you use a smaller float and less lead than would otherwise be necessary, or even to fish with float tackle when you would otherwise have to leger.

Rivers aren't the only waters where you can exploit rush beds. Whenever I'm after tench in summer, I like to find a bed of rushes or reeds and either fish alongside it from the bank, or sit in an anchored boat and fish in towards it.

I often find a nice little gap in a rush bed where I can fish from the bank, and it is interesting to note that there is always a best side. Either you get all the fish with your tackle cast close to the rushes on your right, or else when you're fishing close to those on the left.

I know this, because I often share such a gap with a friend and one or the other gets nearly all the fish. So until you know which is the favoured side, it pays to try them alternately.

Rudd love reed beds, and even in winter, when they prefer deeper water, you'll find them along reed-lined margins where the bottom shelves steeply. As with perch you'll often find it essential to get your bait as close to the stems as possible.

On one Lincolnshire lake where I fish, there are plenty of beautiful rudd between 1lb and 2½lb, but we can only catch them by casting a bait, or a leaded nymph on fly tackle, right in between the reed stems.

They won't come out, even a couple of feet, to take a bait.

Carp too

Carp, too, like reeds and rushes, and if you are hardy enough to fish for carp in winter, try to find places which were either rush-beds or water-lily beds in summer, and put your bait right in the middle.

In these places the bottom will be covered with brown, dead leaves, either of rush or lilies, and no doubt these harbour a good deal of fish food. Carp, when they do decide to feed in winter, are liable to explore these places.

So many anglers spoil, or at any rate, reduce their chances by choosing featureless open stretches of water, where there are few fish because there is no shelter and, in winter, very little feed. Fish are wild animals and behave exactly like other wild animals, in many respects.

If there's a mouse in your house, he doesn't sit in the middle of the room; he runs round close to the walls. If you watch rabbits, you'll find them feeding close along the hedge or the edge of the copse or spinney. So it is with fish. Seek them where there is both food and shelter, and there you will usually find them.

21 December 1972

Is float-fishing neglected?

Most people think a float is no more and no less than a bite indicator. In fact, it is much more. It lets you put enough lead on your tackle to make casting possible, to the distance you need to cast, without the tackle weighing anything once it's in the water.

It also allows the bait to be carried, in running water, farther than you would be able to cast, or alternatively, to be carried by the current quietly to where the fish are, without scaring them by the splash of its arrival.

And it lets you present your bait at whatever depth you decide is correct.

Nowadays, we find a wide range of beautifully made floats, with all sorts of different shapes, sizes and colours. Many of them have advantages for special kinds of fishing and only a few are badly designed.

This enormous choice can be baffling for beginners, and so can the problems of shotting them correctly. Which is a pity, because it leads to the use of complicated design for the wrong job, or to failure of the right float through wrong shotting.

Thirty years ago, the range of floats was much more limited. You could buy crow quills, with or without cork bodies; goose quills; porcupine quills in various sizes; and what were called Thames floats; porcupine quill top, wooden bottom, cork body.

Goose quills
There were also Nottingham sliders. These were cork-bodied goose quills with slider rings, and the rings were always far too big.

Finally, there were celluloid floats of various sizes, with and without antennae.

People managed to catch fish successfully with these; and it is true to say that the very considerable increase in the number of big fish caught, during the last twenty-five years or so, stemmed not so much from any improvement in float design, or from the immense increase in the number of different kinds of float available, but rather from the greater willingness of anglers to fish without any float at all.

It is somewhat paradoxical that at a time when the percentage of fishing done without any float is higher than it has ever been, there should be more and better floats on sale than ever before.

Twenty years ago, those of us who realised that legering or paternostering could often catch more fish, and especially bigger fish, in some conditions, had an uphill job trying to persuade anglers generally that this was so.

In those days, if you watched a National Championship match, you'd find every competitor float-fishing.

I shall never forget a pathetic letter I had from a reader who told me he had been dropped from his club's National Championship team because two members of the selection committee had 'caught him legering'.

Nowadays, the balance has perhaps swung too far. I see anglers using swing tips or other rod-tip indicators to fish in conditions where a simple float tackle would do far better.

Strong case

In some cases, conditions have changed, too. Twenty years ago there were fewer carp-fishers. Carp, if you could get them to bite at all, did so very decisively and you needed no sensitive indicator to tell you about it.

Nowadays, with so many more carp-fishers on the scene, and such a lot of carp being caught and returned, or hooked and lost, bites are often quite finicky.

I could give other examples where float fishing gave place to legering, paternostering, or freeline, fishing, but is now due for a partial comeback.

I'd advise anyone interested in this to avoid getting caught up in abstruse technicalities because, as I have said before in this column, at least 90 per cent of float-fishing can be done just as well with a selection of simple bird quills as it can with a wide range of sophisticated float patterns.

Any angler who has a few each of crow, duck, goose, turkey and swan quills will seldom find himself handicapped in any way at all. And for anyone who goes regularly into the country, such quills are not difficult to obtain.

It is seldom indeed that I spend a day fishing without picking up anything from one to a dozen suitable quills and it would have to be an exceptionally clumsy and unskilful person who couldn't make a useful float from a bird quill.

For those who can't be bothered, I'd recommend stocking up with the simpler shop-style floats, and only buying the special purpose ones when the need for them arises.

Most of the time, you need ask yourself only two questions about a float; 'Will it carry the shot I need to use?' and 'Can I see it easily at the distance at which I shall be fishing?' If the answer is yes to both questions the float will usually do well enough.

As for shotting, there's more nonsense talked about this than about any other aspect of fishing. I've even seen diagrams showing shot-spacings to the nearest sixteenth of an inch, and using three or four sizes of shot.

I only ever carry three sizes, swan, BB and a small shot weighing a quarter as much as a BB. And it is only rarely that I spread out the shot. Nine times out of ten they're bunched together at one place on the line.

Exception

The only exception I can think of, offhand, is when I want the most sensitive possible lift tackle with an antenna float. I then put on as much shot as the float can carry without cocking properly, close up below the float; and the rest of the shot just, but only just, enough to take the float under, all together at the proper distance from the hook. This may be anything from $1/2$ inch to 18 inches.

Believe me, it's only when I'm up against exceptionally shy biters that I find anything of this sort necessary. Even nowadays, with so much pressure on most of our fisheries, that is rare indeed.

Match fishing, in which I'm not involved, poses more problems. A match is usually fished at the worst possible time of day, on a water heavily and regularly hammered by people who catch great numbers of small fish and return them. Numbers of people pound along the banks, causing great vibration, in full view of the fish.

In these circumstances, a little roach or bream of 8 or 9 inches is a wily little beggar. He's had a few years of experience and he remembers his troubles.

I can well imagine that he'd need every trick in the book including fine line, tiny hooks, small baits, and ultra sensitive bite indicators (floats or other devices) to beat him.

If you want to know how to catch such fish, read Ivan Marks and other intelligent matchmen. I'm better at telling you how to avoid tiddlers than how to catch them.

For good fish, simple floats, simply shotted, will nearly always do the job, provided you get all the rest of the fishing right.

5 July 1973

Some like it hot!

As I write, the temperature is over 90 degrees in the shade. But owing to what is known as the botheration factor, or something like that, if I write about fishing in heatwave conditions, it will then turn cold and start to rain before my article gets into print.

Well, we need some rain, don't we? So let's see if I can bring it on.

The hotter the water, the less oxygen it holds. If the dissolved oxygen falls too low, it puts fish off feeding. If you can, fish at the time of day when it is coolest, in the hot weather. That means late evening, through the night where possible, and early morning.

But not everyone can fish at such times. What do you do if you can only fish in the heat of the day? The answer is, seek places where most oxygen is likely to be, and fish for species that are least affected by warm water.

Obvious spots
Below weirs, waterfalls and rapids, there is more oxygen, so these are obvious spots to fish. Don't be afraid to fish in broken water,

where the river foams over rocks or boulders. It may look as if no fish could live in it, but they can and in hot weather, they do, especially barbel, chub and trout.

In ponds and lakes, remember that weeds give out oxygen and fish stay near them when water temperatures are high. Or, if the lake is deep, fish may go down to where the water is cooler. I've pulled trout and perch up from 40 feet, and other species from water nearly as deep.

As well as disliking water that is too hot, some fish avoid bright light. Tench, particularly, move into deeper water as light gets brighter. If a small lake has no cool depths, they have to put up with bright light and swim near the top where there is most oxygen, but otherwise, down they go to where the light is dimmer and the water cooler.

The species of fish that seem least bothered by warm water are rudd and chub. They'll often feed in the middle of a sweltering hot day when nothing else will. Next most likely to bite are dace.

Not many . . .
I suppose I should mention eels. It's never too hot to catch those, but with due respect to the National Anguilla Club, not many people want to catch them.

I don't mind admitting that on days so hot that I couldn't catch anything else except a few gudgeon or bleak, I've had fine sport with eels, using the little fish as dead baits. In fact, the biggest eel I ever caught weighing 5¾lb, was taken in the middle of a very hot day.

You sometimes need unorthodox methods, even to catch the fish most likely to bite in hot weather. I'm not sure if it is right to call fly-fishing unorthodox, but few anglers realise how useful it can be for coarse fish at all times, but more so in a heatwave.

Eyed hook
In such conditions, you may find chub, rudd and even roach lying just under the surface, often in the shade of a tree. If you bang a float tackle or a leger right in the middle of them, they won't like it a bit. But a fly can be dropped with hardly any disturbance. So can a bunch of maggots cast on fly tackle, using a bare eyed hook instead of fly.

113

I can't say that I've caught many really big chub on a fly, though I've had some 5 pounders. But I've had more on free-line tackle and floating baits, mainly breadcrust or flake, allowed to drift down the current to where the chub were lying.

Of course, you can also catch chub by dapping, as Izaak Walton explained. In fact, his advice about dapping for chub is about the only thing he didn't pinch from a previous author, as far as we know. I wouldn't even bet that he didn't pinch it from someone, anyway.

Beetles . . .

I wonder if the Izaak Waltons of today, the writers that live on ideas they pinch from others, will be as much praised in 300 years from today as Walton is now?

But I digress. You don't need grasshoppers or slugs for dapping, though both are good baits, as are beetles, bumblebees, worms and other creatures. But bread is just as good.

If you don't fancy getting stung, you can make a very realistic artificial bumblebee, with an underbody of polyethylene foam wound over with clipped ostrich herl; wings of barred black and white cock hackle, legs of any strong black feather fibre with a knot in each fibre. It'll float like a haystack, and chub really love it. So, occasionally, do trout. Tie it with a No 6 hook.

There are tricks you can try in hot weather, provided you don't let them disturb or annoy fellow anglers. Putting a drag through a pitch in a pond or lake may colour up the water temporarily, and stir up enough of the creatures that live in the bottom mud to attract one or two tench.

Stir up

And if you're river fishing, you can go upstream of a likely spot, and stir up the bottom with your boots, or your landing net handle, or a stray branch or hedge-stake. That can attract various kinds of fish, especially barbel and perch.

Hot weather separates the real anglers from the others. It puts a premium on thinking and on willingness to be unorthodox. It's no good just sitting, sweating and catching nothing.

You have to scout around, find where the fish are, and often enough, use methods very different from what you would choose in normal conditions. On rivers, poke around in the sidestreams, and the heavily bushed areas. Look for the weirs, the falls and the broken water. On still waters, think before you pick a pitch.

14 July 1976

Keep your cool!

With autumn moving to winter, it's time for me to repeat what I've written before about the effects of temperature, light, current and water colour on the feeding of fish.

When the water temperature falls below the critical temperature of 39.2°F, there is a drastic change in the behaviour of freshwater fish. The faster the temperature falls, and the lower it goes, the greater the effect, but in any case the figure of 39.2°F is critical.

Immediately after the temperature has fallen below it, fish eat a great deal less, and in rivers they tend to move out of the main current and into the slow or slack water.

In big lakes, they move into deeper water as the temperature falls, and if a lake is deep enough, they can find areas where the temperature never gets below about 42°F, all through the winter. In such waters, they can always avoid water below that critical 39.2°F, and if you can find them and get a bait to them, you can catch them.

In the shallower lakes and ponds, and in rivers, the fish can't avoid being in water below 39.2°F. After they've been in it for several days, they start feeding again, though never as freely as they do in warmer weather.

I've been asked why fish won't feed at times, even in bright, sun shiny days when it is warm enough on the bank to cause anglers to take their coats off. Well, the answer is that a spell of sunny autumn and winter days is associated with clear nights, and clear nights mean high temperature loss. The fall in water temperature at night is not fully restored by the sunshine on the following day. You may be sitting there on the bank, enjoying the warmth of the sun; but stick a thermometer in the water, and it will show you that although you may feel warm, the fish don't.

115

An early picture of the author fishing the Bedfordshire Ivel during a snowstorm

Light

Remember, however, that if you're fishing a deep lake, with areas of bottom below 20 feet or so, sunshine is very welcome. On a dull day, there isn't much light below 20 feet, but if the sun shines, the light level down there is much higher.

Now, just as some fish feed very little when the light is too bright, others don't feed much if it isn't bright enough. Perch are the chaps that like enough light – remember, you don't catch many after dusk in the summer, do you? All right, if you know a deep lake holding big perch, bless the autumn and winter sunshine that provides enough light in the deep holes to start them feeding. Pike, too, though to a lesser extent.

The fish that don't like too much light are affected just as much in autumn and winter as they are in summer. Roach, for example, may keep you waiting till the light begins to fall before they'll bite freely, whether it is June or December. I've caught them after dark in winter, when there have been no bites in daylight.

What do you do if the water is below 39.2°F, and there are no areas of water that you can find where it is warmer?

First, find slow or slack water. Second rig tackle that will stay put where you cast it, but which can be moved to cover an area of bottom. Third, though this isn't an invariable rule, use smaller baits than usual. Fourth, use very little groundbait.

Sluggish

The fish don't want much food. So don't fill their very limited capacity with groundbait. Nor do they feel inclined to dash about. So you must move your bait to them, but very slowly, so as to give them time to take it without their having to move quickly.

And fifth, use sensitive tackle that lets you detect delicate bites, because, delicate bites are what you'll be most likely to get. You move your bait, a little at a time, letting it dither between each move. Eventually, it comes close to the fish, so that he can suck it in. He does, but he isn't going anywhere. He's sluggish. You're not going to see much of a bite indication, are you?

That is why you need sensitive tackle.

Water colour has two effects.

It deludes anglers into thinking the fish can't see them, so they stand bolt upright, getting between water and sky. The fish are scared, because no matter how little light reaches them, if there's any at all, it will be reduced if an angler gets between the fish and the sky. They can't actually see you, but they know you're there.

Imagine you're in a room that has frosted glass windows. If someone passes a window, you know it don't you? Right, fish know if you pass their window, so don't do it.

Water is never as coloured as it looks. It can appear to be little better than mud, but dip out a jam jar full and you'll be surprised.

The other effect of coloured water is to reduce light penetration. That may cause such fish as roach to feed in brighter general light conditions than they would feed in if the water were clearer. It may also prevent perch or pike from feeding because it cuts out too much light.

Coloured water affects different rivers in different ways. Provided the temperature isn't too low, some colour in rivers that are mainly rain-fed, and that includes the Thames and the Ouse, will often cause fish to feed quite keenly. The same amount of colour in a spring-fed river, such as the Hampshire Avon or the Test, will put fish right off. It takes a good deal of practical fishing experience to enable an angler to judge the effects of colour in the rivers he fishes.

Colour in the water puts a premium on worms for bait. It's logical, after all. Colour in the water is usually caused by an increasing current, or a rise in the water, washing soil from the banks.

One effect of very cold water that is often overlooked is its effect on baits. Worms will wriggle in water so cold that maggots are rigid, and pastes become considerably stiffer, specially cheese paste; so if you expect to fish in very cold water, mix your paste much softer. There's a case for using casters instead of maggots, but the advantage of maggots, even without wriggle, is that you can see if you've had a bite without any indication, because your maggot comes up with its inside missing. Then you know you're fishing in the right place.

1 *December 1976*

118

PART IV
TACKLE

Does the answer lie in the nylon?

As is now well known, lots of barbel, including some big ones, have been caught from the Dorset Stour by anglers using one or two grains of hempseed on hooks as big as No 6, which seems to show that some kinds of fish are not scared of seeing hooks.

Yet we often find cases where reducing the size of the hook appears to make all the difference between catching fish and failing to do so. A few weeks ago, a member of a club at whose evening meeting I was invited to speak, asked me if I could explain how it was that the bream went off feed in a swim he was fishing with maggots on a No 14 hook, but when he changed to a 16 he began catching them again.

There are, of course, many possible explanations. The shoal from which he caught his first fish may have moved off, and another arrived shortly after he had changed his hook. Or the same shoal moved off and returned. Or something temporarily scared them.

Be that as it may, we all know that there are cases where changing to a smaller hook produces bites we weren't getting before; at any rate it seems to do so.

I wonder whether it is the change in hook size that produces the bites, or whether some other change has been made at the same time. Sometimes, of course, the change of hook is accompanied by a decrease in the size of the bait, but that cannot apply when the bait is maggot or some kind of seed.

Much more likely to make a difference is the reduction in stiffness of the nylon to which the hook is attached. Almost always, if you buy whipped-on hooks you will find that the smaller the size, the thinner the nylon. Now, I've raised the question of nylon size before, saying that I doubt very much if fish are scared by the sight of nylon, except perhaps those that have learned to associate it with an uncomfortable experience, like getting caught.

Actually, I'm inclined to doubt whether fish associate getting caught with nylon, or with hooks, leads or floats. It seems much more likely that they associate it with the particular kind of bait they took. Please don't write and tell me they don't associate it with anything, because if there's one thing I'm certain of about fish, it is that they often learn from a single experience to avoid certain baits or lures.

The bait's behaviour

If that is so, why then should using thinner nylon produce more bites? Well, I'm convinced that although fish aren't suspicious of the nylon itself, they can detect its effect on the bait. The behaviour of a maggot, or kernel of wheat, or a bit of crust or flake, may be very different when it is on a hook attached to nylon from when it isn't.

If it's tethered to a lead, or a bunch of shot, it won't sink in the same way, or follow the current as naturally as when it's free. Even when there's no shot or float on the line, the water resistance on the nylon will affect the behaviour of the bait.

You may say 'That's all very well, but you can't tell me that changing from six thou' nylon to five thou' will make any difference. Fish can't measure nylon to a thousandth of an inch!'

You'll be surprised when I tell you how much difference a thou' makes in this particular case. Not to water resistance; that only decreases by about 16 per cent, which, however, is perhaps more than you thought.

No, what decreases startlingly is the stiffness of the nylon. Five thou' nylon has less than half the stiffness of six thou'.

Well, perhaps you don't believe it, but it's true. The stiffness varies with the fourth power of the diameter. And a change in stiffness of two to one will make a very considerable difference in the way in which a bait can behave naturally or otherwise, specially when it is allied to a reduction of 16 per cent in water resistance.

There it is, then. A bait on five thou' nylon is much freer to move naturally, than if it is on six thou' stuff. Enough to make all the difference between fish taking or refusing a bait, sometimes.

That is why what may seem a small improvement in a monofilament line can make a lot of difference. If the chemists find a way to make a new kind of nylon as strong in the five thou' thickness as earlier kinds were in the six thou' size, the gain is much more than in mere strength. It means that on the new nylon, the bait can move more than twice as freely for the same tackle strength.

Of course, that isn't the only way to obtain an improvement. The chemists may be able to find a kind of nylon that isn't any stronger for a given thickness, but which is more flexible. That too would give us a considerable advantage.

Don't underestimate advantages of this sort. None of us ever knows how many fish have a good look at our baits and then refuse them, when they would have taken them had they behaved more naturally. None of us knows how many fish take our baits, feel the stiffness of the nylon, and spit out the bait again without registering on the float or whatever other means of detecting bites we may be using. We don't know how many; but I'd bet if it would be known, that over a season it adds up to far more fish than we succeed in catching.

Others turn away

Look at the number of times you pull up your tackle only to find a fish attached, or to find the bait marked in such a way that it must have been in a fish's mouth. That's just the ones that sampled it; what about all those that turned away?

Let me make it clear that I'm not advocating that every angler should change to thinner nylon, regardless of the size and fighting power of the fish he is after or the existence of weeds and snags. It is silly to hook fish after fish that your tackle is altogether too feeble to land. Better hook fewer and land more.

What is worth knowing is how great a difference can be made by what seems a small change in the thickness of the nylon, and more important, how valuable improved kinds of nylon can be, whatever the strength our judgment tells us is suitable for the kind of fishing we are doing.

Just a cautionary note. In fly-fishing, you cannot make much use of finer nylons of better strength except perhaps at the very tip of the leader. This is because you need weight to make the leader straighten, and most nylon leaders are already too light to cast well. Making them thinner for the same strength doesn't help because that would only make them lighter still.

Part of the reason why most of them are too light is because if they're made any thicker to get more weight, they become too stiff. It's a complete fallacy that stiffness is advantageous in a leader. If it's heavy enough it cannot be too flexible.

What would help would be new nylons that were more flexible

for a given thickness. Then we could go thicker and therefore heavier, on parts of the leader, without sacrificing flexibility.

Of course, the one thing we can afford to sacrifice least is reliability!

23 December 1966

Swim-feeders

In the last few weeks I have been experimenting with swim-feeders. I must admit that although I have tried them from time to time in the past, I've never been entirely happy about their use, though I know they have led to good catches of many kinds of fish.

The trouble about swim-feeders is that if they're big enough to hold enough maggots to act as a real attraction to the fish you want to catch, they're too heavy to cast properly. They offer too much resistance to the strike, and are liable to get jammed under weed or snags. If they're small enough to avoid the handicaps, they don't hold enough maggots.

However, the people who make and sell swim-feeders have struck what seems to me a sensible compromise in the matter and if my experience is any guide, there's nothing to gain by making swim-feeders much bigger or much smaller than those you can buy in the shops.

What is more important is how you use these things.

Weight
First of all, there is the question of weight. With any form of legering, it is important to get the weight right. In still water, you want as little weight as possible; in running water you want just enough weight to hold bottom and no more. Many chances are missed because a fish feels weight or drag or both and drops the bait before the angler can strike.

Not everyone agrees with me, but I think that more fish turn downstream after taking the bait, than move upstream with it.

Now you cannot, in running water, rig your leger or swim-feeder tackle to suit the fish that moves upstream. Such a fish will not register a bite until he is upstream of your lead or feeder, by the length of your hook link. If he moves farther than that, you'll soon get the feel of the lead or the feeder shifting, or see a cross-current movement of the line. It won't be a slack-line bite, except perhaps in a very slow current, because the drag of the current on the line will keep it in a state of tension, and obviously a fish producing the indication must be feeling not only the weight of the lead or feeder but also the drag on the line by the current.

Don't tell me that the fish can pull line through the ring or swivel of the lead or feeder without moving it. Try a bit of under-water testing and you'll find the lead or the feeder will always move if you pull on the hook, upstream or down, unless its weight is al-together excessive; and then the friction of the line through the ring or swivel is plenty for the fish to feel.

Face the fact that an upstream-moving fish that has taken your bait has a good chance of being missed and there isn't a thing you can do about it.

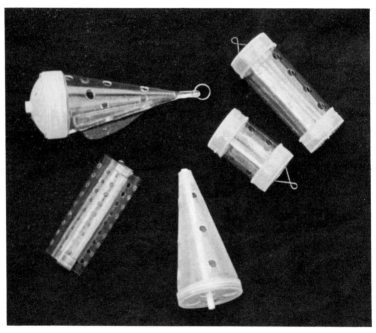

A selection of swimfeeders — conical, block-end and open-end (Angling Times)

Fortunately, most fish turn downstream after taking a bait, as I have said. If the lead or feeder is just and only just heavy enough to hold bottom in the current, then the downstream-moving fish will feel almost no drag. You'll get a good bite indication and you shouldn't miss too many chances. If you do, it either means you are using too much weight or that the fish are feeling the rod top.

Since current speeds vary considerably, it follows that the weight of a swim-feeder ought to be adjustable. A feeder with a fixed strip of lead can't be right for all conditions. In practice, such feeders are too heavy for most conditions. I think it better to do away with lead strips and instead, to have a short length of nylon attached to one end of the feeder on to which you can nip as many swan shot as are necessary to hold bottom – and only just hold – in the swim you're fishing.

The other end of the feeder should carry a swivel, so that if the hook-length twists round the line above the feeder, it can untwist as the tackle sinks. That was the object of using a swivel in Arlesey bombs and it works well in practice.

The possible exception to the principle of using as lightly loaded a feeder as possible, is in certain barbel swims, where there is reason for thinking that some barbel which hardly ever move upstream after taking the bait, will hook themselves against the weight and drag of a big heavy feeder. I am sure this does happen.

What I am not so sure about is whether the use of such a feeder catches more barbel than would be taken with a minimum-weight feeder used by an angler who holds his rod and feels for bites. Remember that while a good emphatic pull is a common kind of barbel bite, there are times, and they are not rare, when barbel bites take the form of a trembling or vibration which no kind of visible bite indicator can detect.

Resting
I say emphatically, that any angler who relies on a swing-tip, spring-tip, quiver-tip or butt indicator, leaving his rod supported by a rest cannot hope to catch barbel as consistently as the man who holds his rod in one hand and the line between butt-ring and reel between the fingers of the other. It is by feel and feel alone that this kind of barbel bite can be detected, yet when you do detect it, the following strike hardly ever fails to connect.

Swim-feeders come in two shapes, cylindrical and conical. I can't say I've found that there is any advantage in one compared to the other. The ideal shape, which isn't available, would be the same as an Arlesey bomb, ie streamlined.

One way of obtaining the same effect as a swim-feeder, but with less obstruction to the strike, is the use of nylon net bags of a mesh that allows maggots to escape at the right rate. This is important because if the rate is too high, you can get through a very large quantity of maggots in a short time. Last time I was fishing, I used a gallon in five hours.

Regardless of how good the swim-feeder is for attracting fish to the baited hook, it does serve one important purpose, that of encouraging its users to fish actively, instead of casting out and waiting for a bite for very long periods, often with the hook bait concealed, or caught up, or sucked to empty skins by small dace, gudgeon or roach. You soon learn how long a feeder takes to empty and as soon as you think it has emptied, you retrieve and reload it. That way, you never lose much time because of a hidden or snagged hook, or an unattractive bait.

Swallowed

One problem I haven't solved is that of big fish, barbel and chub mainly, taking the whole swim-feeder instead of the baited hook. I actually watched one crafty, old chub do this. He picked up the swim-feeder between his lips and shot off downstream with it nearly taking the rod out of my hand. If I hadn't been able to see what had happened, I should have wondered how I could have missed such a positive bite.

I fancy this happens more often than most users of swim-feeders realise on waters that hold barbel and chub. Maybe, when it is suspected, we should dispense with a hook-length and attach a bigger hook to a small swim-feeder instead!

If you want the best results from swim-feeders, it pays to transfer your maggots from sawdust to bran. No fish likes eating sawdust, while bran blows away as you load the feeder. I can never understand why maggots are sold in sawdust, anyway, though perhaps the maggot breeders have good reason. Bran is cheap enough, surely?

23 November 1973

Keep shot simple

Ever since I started fishing at a tender age, I've been puzzled by the arrangement of shot that anglers use for float-fishing. I still am.

To understand what I'm driving at, let's consider a simple float made of peacock quill, about the same thickness throughout its length. We will assume that for every BB shot on the line, this float will sit one inch deeper in the water.

Therefore, to pull this float down one inch, a fish will have to apply a pull equal to the weight of a BB shot in water. And to make the float rise one inch, the fish will have to carry the weight of a BB shot in water.

It won't make the least difference where the shot are placed on the line below the float. It won't even make any difference what sort of shot they are.

Suppose we decide to fish with this float, using it for the lift method. In that case, we pinch on a swan shot, equivalent in weight to 4 BBs. It rests on the bottom and the float is cocked, with, say, half an inch of top showing above the surface.

To make that top rise one inch, a fish will still have to carry the weight of one BB shot. It will lift the swan shot, but it won't have to carry the weight of the swan shot. If the float rises one inch, it will carry the weight of 3 BBs itself. That is, three-quarters of the weight of the swan shot. The fish will carry the other quarter, ie 1 BB.

Now! If we put 3 BBs close under the float, and 1 BB near the hook, we shall not, as many anglers seem to think, make the least difference to the weight the fish has to lift to make the float rise one inch. Nor shall we have improved the sensitivity of the rig in any way whatever.

It'll be just the same, whatever arrangement of shot we use, or however we distribute them, or whatever size of shot we use, provided they add up to the same total weight.

What about inertia? Well, again it makes no difference how the shot are distributed, in practical fishing. If a fish pulls the float down, it will have to move all the shot, and it's their total weight that counts, not their sizes or distribution.

Then there is water resistance. That is at its least if you use one large shot rather than several smaller ones. But if you use several, the water resistance will be less if they're bunched than if they are spread out.

There are special cases where you need the shot to consist of more than one, and to be spread instead of being bunched. If you want to drag bottom, you need a shot of the right size nearest the hook. What that size is depends on depth, current speed and type of bottom. And to drag properly, you'll need a float that carries more than that one shot nearest the hook.

Extra shot

But there's no advantage in spreading these extra shot. You may just as well put them in a bunch, somewhere between that bottom shot and the float. Exactly where you put them depends on how fast you want your tackle to go down.

In a fast short swim you'd put them within about 6 inches of the bottom shot. You might also do that in slower water if you wanted to get past shoals of bleak or small dace that were concentrated near the surface or at midwater.

If you're casting a long way across open water, it often pays to concentrate the shot near the hook so they fly ahead of the float and prevent the hook catching over the line above the float. But if you're trying to fish close against the far bank, or as near as possible to the bed or rush or reeds, you can concentrate the shot – or all but one of them – against the bottom of the float.

Small price

The float is cast where you want it to be and the tackle, as it sinks, will swing underneath it.

With that arrangement, you'll find the hook catches above the float now and then, and you'll have to wind in and disentangle it. But that's a small price to pay for putting your bait where it will catch fish.

What is often very important is the distance between the bottom shot and the hook. The longer you make it, the more naturally the bait behaves in the water, but the slower the tackle will be to register a bite, unless the biting fish moves straight away from the float. Conversely, the closer you put your bottom shot to the hook, the sooner a bite will be registered, but the bait will not behave as naturally – unless it is on the bottom – and the sooner a fish will feel the weight of the shot, which may cause it to eject the bait.

There are no hard and fast rules for deciding just how far from the hook the bottom shot should be, except in lift-method fishing, when the shot is about one inch from the hook. Otherwise, it's a question of trial and error.

If you think fish are ejecting the bait because they're feeling the shot before you can strike, move the shot farther from the hook. If you think fish are refusing the bait because it is behaving unnaturally, again move the shot farther from the hook.

If you're after fish feeding off bottom, specially in still or slow water, you may decide to put one fairly small shot within 6 inches to a foot from the hook, and the rest of the shot close to the float. The float will then cock at once when you cast, but sink a little deeper when the shot near the hook has sunk all the way. This secondary sinking is easier to see with an antenna float.

You soon assess how long it takes for the bottom shot to sink. If the float doesn't settle a bit deeper at the time you know it should, it means a fish has intercepted the sinking bait. So you tighten.

Near hook

But remember, special cases are not very commonly needed. I do most of my float-fishing with all the shot bunched in one place, and usually, a few big shot rather than a greater number of smaller ones. Nine times out of ten, these shot are a foot to 18 inches from the hook and I seem to catch fish very successfully.

I am sure that most inexperienced anglers become hopelessly confused with all the advice they read about float types and shot distributions. Most of the time, they'd do better to stick to the simple floats and simple shottings that I use.

I'm not alone in favouring this simplicity, either. Most of the men who catch big fish regularly adopt the same procedure. If you want to exercise your mind, use it on problems of where and when to fish, and what baits to use.

5 May 1976

Golden oldies with the pole!

I've been very interested to see how much the pole has gained popularity, especially in match-fishing circles.

I began using a pole, or rather, some of a pole, in 1923! That was because one of my grandfathers, who lived at Hertford, had two Sowerbutts poles, with which he fished for roach in the Lee.

As soon as I was old enough to go fishing, I was given the upper two pieces of the older of the two poles. As I grew, I had three pieces, then four, then the whole pole.

Those poles were bored out from wood or bamboo to a very thin wall-thickness then whipped at close intervals to prevent splitting. Everything possible was done to save weight, but despite this, the old poles weighed from 32 to 36oz for an 18 footer, and what with the leverage of so long a rod, they took some handling.

Big fish

But we did handle them, very successfully, because we were taught how to do so by the experts. There really were experts in those days. I've see quite big fish, 4lb chub, 4lb tench and even a 6lb barbel, landed on roach poles.

The first lesson I had was how to hold the pole. Your box, stool or basket (the Lee pole experts favoured a black-painted wooden box, with a padded lid covered with what was called American cloth – it was waterproof) had to be just the right height, so that when you sat on it, your thighs were horizontal.

Then, the box had to be placed correctly – not square on to the bank, but at an angle. You sat, if you were right-handed, with your thighs making an angle of about 60° to one another and the right thigh parallel to the bank.

Your left forearm lay on your left thigh, left hand near the knee, palm up, and its finger tips supported the pole, whose butt lay across your right thigh, gripped by the right hand, thumb along the top and fingers underneath.

The whole of the right forearm lay along the pole, whose butt projected only an inch or so beyond the right elbow.

When we fished hemp, with a tiny porcupine float shotted to just show its tip at the surface, and a very short topping (the piece of line between float and pole-tip) we struck with the left ankle!

Yes, it's true – you simply lifted your left heel, keeping the ball of the foot on the ground. The tip of the pole went up a foot and the fish was usually hooked.

Nobody used elastic in those days, but the top 12 to 18 inches of the pole was very flexible indeed. Some were made of whalebone. Ah, you may say, but much stronger tackle was used then – now we use ¾lb bs nylon.

Don't believe it! Many of the expert Lee roach fishers used horsehair, and one old chap I knew used human hair, and caught roach over the pound on that, regularly.

'Yer cawn't beat 'uming 'air, son', he used to say, 'if ony yer can learn ter 'endle it!'

Even those who used silkworm gut fished very fine indeed – the size was 8x which would be less than 1lb bs.

Flexible

I'm inclined to think that what saved breakage was the very flexible tip and the method of holding the pole. That allowed great control of striking. As I've explained, the left ankle did it when you fished a short topping. With a longer one, the left-hand fingers did a bit as well, but unless you actually lifted the back of that left hand from where it rested on your left knee, you simply couldn't strike too hard.

Lately, I've seen quite a lot of photographs of anglers using poles and their method seems to me curious. I'd probably have got a clip round the ear from my grandfather if I'd allowed the butt of the pole to stick out a yard behind my back, with my right hand extended backwards to grip it – or if that hadn't happened, I'd have had that rearward extension run into by somebody cycling along the narrow towpath from which we usually fished.

If a yard or more of the pole is going to stick out behind the angler, he might as well take off the butt section and save weight!

I'm often asked whether I prefer take-apart or telescopic poles. Well, all the old poles were of the take-apart kind and I prefer that kind. I have a telescopic pole, and it works quite well, but if I were a matchman, I'd go for the take-apart sort every time. It's quicker to change length with it.

Some of the latest poles are around 33 feet long, and I'm inclined to doubt their efficiency. Even in carbon fibre, there must be quite a lot of delay in tightening on a bite because of reverse flex, and I'd hate to have to control such a thing in a stiff cross-wind. I take my hat off to anyone who can do that successfully!

I was always taught that a pole gave best results when you could pick a swim that was really well suited to it – where you could lower the tackle into the water with the least possible disturbance and keep the tip of the pole straight above the float all the time.

Using a longer topping to reach out farther was frowned on by the old Lee experts. Certainly, nothing beats a pole for reducing disturbance, provided you can reach your fish without swinging the tackle out.

Dreaded

What we always dreaded when using the pole was being 'pointed'. That meant a fish pulling so that the line and the pole were both in line and there was no spring in the top of the pole to cushion a jerk. Being 'pointed' nearly always meant being broken, so you did your best to keep the pole-tip directly above your fish.

In fairly deep water, with roach, bream, tench and barbel, you usually managed that, but with chub, or with almost any big fish in shallow water, it was difficult. That first dash of a big chub caused many a smash. The other thing you had to avoid was being too eager to disjoint the pole and land the fish.

Now and then a fish would come fast straight at the angler and I've known that to smash the top of the pole, but mostly either the top stood up to it, specially if it was whalebone, or else the tackle broke.

Where the pole really scored was in its ability to fish very soft baits. You could fish a square of what the old hands called golden breadcrust, which was so soft that it simply couldn't be cast, not even a little way.

With the pole, it was gently lowered and stayed on the hook. Very soft paste could be and was used, too, stuff so soft that the least jerk would make it fall off, but the pole handled it perfectly.

With fish in popular match waters becoming more and more educated to the dangers of maggots, casters and bloodworms, it might be worth trying some of those baits that the old Lee pole experts used with such success. *15 October 1980*

Easy to swallow

There are two terms that one hears used often by specimen hunters and pike fishers – 'bite-offs' and 'gut-hooking'.

The first occurs when a fish that has throat-teeth (pharyngeals) swallows the bait, usually without giving sufficient indication to cause the angler to strike, and then bites off the nylon above the hook.

This happens most commonly when particle baits like sweet-corn, tares, various beans and other small baits are fished in an area where a good deal of the same stuff has been spread over a small area.

A fish that has picked up, say, a grain of corn, and has plenty of other similar grains within a few inches, continues to mop them up without moving far. Consequently, there is no positive bite indication.

Cheese

It doesn't only happen with small particle baits, however. I've known chub do it with lumps of cheese as big as a pigeon's egg, or with big slugs, small dead fish, and other big baits. All fish with throat teeth, and that means all the carp family, can do it, and do do it at times.

When we wind in and find maggots reduced to skins, or worms well and truly chewed, we know that teeth were responsible. And, with such fish as roach, rudd, dace, bream, tench, barbel and carp, that means that we escaped a bite-off by only a fraction of an inch. The biting fish has almost swallowed the bait – had it done so completely, there would very likely have been a bite-off.

Gut-hooking of pike is also due to the bait having been swallowed. There is no bite-off because pike don't have throat teeth and we use wire traces. And of course, gut-hooking of other fish like perch, zander and eels is also due to the bait being swallowed.

Yes, I know I'm stating the obvious, but I have to do so before coming to what may be less obvious. You only get bite-offs or gut-hookings when the hook is in the bait. It doesn't have to be.

Take a look at a 20lb pike, which will be about 40 inches long. How far is its stomach behind its mouth? Twelve inches, perhaps!

133

Very well, suppose we use a 10 inch deadbait like a herring or small mackerel. We don't have to put a hook in the bait. We can use a wire trace ending in a treble, thread a bit of string through the bait from end to end, with a noose over the bait's nose, and then tie the end of the string that comes out of the tail end of the bait, to the treble – leaving a couple of inches of string between hooks and bait.

Now, if a pike swallows that bait right down to his guts, he will get the hook nicely in his mouth. He can't possibly swallow the hook, unless he happens to be a very unusual pike, in the habit of swallowing baits tail-first. With good big deadbaits, that is very rare indeed.

Tighten

The beauty of this arrangement is that you can discriminate between good-sized pike and small ones. The small ones haven't distance enough between mouth and stomach to get the hook into their mouths at all, so you'll miss those when you tighten.

Now, in the last few years there's been a crusade against damaging pike, let alone killing any, which borders on hysteria. It has been much the same with eels. I wonder how many of those who support these crusades will now change to the method I've just described? It will be interesting to see.

A similar method can be used to prevent bite-offs when using particle baits and seeds for such fish as carp, chub and tench. Just find out how far back the throat teeth of the fish you're after are from its lips, and then have the bait on a little string, or cotton thread, so that when it has reached the throat teeth, the hook is just nicely inside the lips of your carp, chub or whatever.

Here again, it'll not avoid bite-offs; it will avoid catching fish smaller than those you're after. It won't give a better bite indication right away, but if the fish that takes your bait can't bite the hook off, it may give some indication before it bites the cotton and even if it doesn't you won't lose your hook.

Missing

Some bite-offs happen without any indication, especially with chub, and you wind in to find the hook missing. Others happen when you've spotted the bite too late, after the bait has been swallowed. The fish is on for a few seconds, then off, and you find a frayed end of nylon instead of a hook. Putting the bait on an extension thread should avoid that sort of bite-off.

I don't think this scheme is of any use in avoiding squashed or sucked maggots, or chewed worms. Only improved bite indication can help there, because the bait has been ejected without the angler knowing about it. The extended-bait system can only work where the fish you're after is willing to swallow the bait and would swallow the hook as well, if it were in the bait, and so bite-off or be hooked in the guts.

Now, I don't claim any credit for this extended-bait idea, because I didn't think it up myself, nor have I been able to try it out enough to assess its potential fully. I heard about it from a friend.

So there you are. If you think the method has possibilities, it's up to you to give it a try and find out for yourself how well it works. That's what I'm going to do, and it will be an extensive trial, not just an hour or two when there's nothing much doing.

10 December 1980

PART V

THE FISH

Why big fish aren't caught

Since it became known that I catch quite a number of specimen fish, all sorts of reasons have been suggested for it. Some of the mistaken ones seem so prevalent that I think I'd better try and explain the way in which I really do fish.

First of all, I haven't any more spare time than most people. I work five days a week in an engineering firm, so, like the majority of anglers, I have summer evenings and week-ends in which to fish – no more.

Every year I have a week's fishing holiday with Maurice Ingham, which we spend in pursuit of the biggest and most difficult fish we know of. Last year I never had a bite, and the year before I only had one during the whole week.

Now and then I am able to fish certain private waters. Like any other keen angler I am glad to have the chance, but I don't have it very often, and at least 80 per cent of my fishing is done on club and ticket waters, which yield most of the specimen fish I catch.

Many tangles

I am far from being skilful for I make lots of bad casts and get just as many tangles as anyone else. I miss plenty of bites and do plenty of other wrong things.

Yet I catch enough big fish for a correspondent to say in *Angling Times* recently that it appears 'something wonderful' to seasoned anglers like himself. What are the reasons for it?

I know very well what the reasons are. They're reasons so simple that I hardly ever dare mention them at the waterside. I see dozens and dozens of anglers fishing with the poorest of chances of catching a decent fish, but if I told them why, they'd be offended.

The only ones I ever dare try to put on the right track are the youngsters. You see they are eager to learn, and not offended if they're told they're fishing wrong.

Now I'm going to try again to explain why most of the anglers I see seldom, if ever, catch a specimen fish.

A stealthy approach can often pay rich dividends for big fish of all species

They're so eager to begin fishing that they don't take the time or trouble to find where the fish are. I spend more time finding fish than fishing for them. They aren't spread throughout a water, like currants in a pudding.

I know that finding the fish isn't always easy. But if you never try, you never learn a thing about how to do it. Anyone can look at a piece of water and ask himself whereabouts he would choose to be if he were a fish, paying attention to current, and depth, and wind, and temperature, and the position of cover, the nature of the bottom, and the natural food.

Often wrong
At first, you're often wrong, but even at first you are right often enough to catch some decent fish, and as time goes on and you start to pile up experience, you're right more and more often.

When I tell a youngster that he can't catch a fish that isn't there, so he must find where the fish are before he tries to catch them, he usually believes me. Older anglers are often so insulted at the suggestion that they're overlooking the obvious that they keep right on overlooking it.

The next most important reason why lots of youngsters don't catch many good fish is that when they do happen to pick the right spot, they proceed to scare all the fish worth catching away. I seldom see an angler who is taking trouble to avoid scaring the fish.

A little while ago I visited a water from which specimen fish are caught, but only now and again. A match was in progress, and, not content with sitting at the water's edge in full view of the fish, at least half the anglers were sitting on stools placed actually in the water, some as much as 6 feet out from the bank.

Very rare
Wherever I go, the sight of an angler who is making any attempt to keep out of sight of the fish, or to avoid causing vibrations that might alarm them is very, very rare.

I don't find any difficulty in convincing youngsters that fish can both see and feel vibrations; that they take fright when they do, and that scared fish won't bite even if they stay in the swim. Young anglers seem to rather enjoy making a stealthy approach to a swim, and keeping concealed when they reach it.

But when I see an older angler tramping along the bank, cutting down any cover that happens to be growing between him and the fish, standing bolt upright at the edge while he assembles his tackle and plumbs the depth, and as often as not wearing a white shirt or something else that fish can see 50 yards away, I daren't say a thing about it to him, even if he's ruined my chances as well as his own, which happens very often. If I did say anything, he wouldn't thank me – he'd be cross.

On top of all that, there are still other reasons why big fish aren't caught. Lots and lots of anglers have made up their minds what tackle they mean to use, and have got it all made up on a winder, before they leave home.

I don't possess any tackle winders. I haven't any use for them. No two swims are alike. No one can say what tackle is needed, or what method of fishing will be best, until he has chosen and carefully studied his swim.

It doesn't take years and years of experience to decide on the right tackle for any swim and any fish you come across.

I hear endless arguments about the relative merits of legering and float fishing, of shot legers and running bullets, etc, etc. One might think that there existed a kind of master tackle and master method which in each and every circumstance would invariably beat everything else. Of course there isn't.

Simple way

There's a very simple way of deciding what to use, which I explain to the youngsters. It is to use the simplest tackle that will catch the fish. Start with the hook, chosen to suit the bait, on a line strong enough to give you a fair chance of landing the fish when you hook it, and only add what is absolutely essential in the way of leads, floats etc.

I can tell this to the youngsters, and they believe it and go and catch fish, but if I try to say the same thing to older men, ten to one they'll say something like 'I'm a leger man myself', or 'I always float-fish – it takes more skill than legering', or 'I've got a favourite float I always use' or 'If I can't catch a fish on 6x I'll stop calling myself an angler!'

This season I've used No 16 hooks on ¾lb bs nylon, a small porcupine, and two dust-shot, to tackle some big roach and dace.

141

I've also used a 9lb bs line, a 1oz Arlesey bomb, and a No 3 eyed hook to fish for big carp. I've used a No 6 on 6lb bs line, without any float or lead to fish for chub; I've used a 5lb line a quill and balsa float carrying 20 BB shot, and a No 6 hook, to trot down 60 yards or more on the Wye.

Sometimes I've caught the fish I wanted, very often I've failed completely, but I should have been lucky indeed to catch any specimens at all if I'd fished the first spot I came to; if I scared all the fish and if I'd used the same tackle all the time.

Main reason

Those are the three main reasons for failing to catch any fish. They're very, very simple and obvious reasons, and if all those chaps who think, quite wrongly, that there's something wonderful about the way I catch specimen fish, would take notice of the simple things, they'd soon find they were catching big fish.

It seems such a pity that with a few exceptions, the only anglers I can convince are schoolboys.

8 July 1955

Chub – a fish of many moods

'The chub,' says my textbook, 'is omnivorous.' Strictly speaking, that means the chub eats everything, and of course we all know that there are very few things that could be considered eatable at all, that chub won't eat. Sometimes, though, chub are very perverse.

In his book of coarse fishing, J. H. R. Bazley tells how he and a friend went chub fishing, groundbaited with cheese and fished with cheese paste for two hours, and, not having had a bite, decided to try for roach instead.

They immediately caught a 5-pound chub and three 4-pounders on maggots – and found cheese groundbait in the mouths of all four fish. Bazley thought that perhaps they hadn't like the 3x gut he'd used to fish the cheese, but didn't mind the 5x he used to fish the maggots.

Peas? No, worm

Several years ago, I used to catch a lot of chub at Offord on peas. Waste peas were tipped into the river at one point and during the summer and early autumn I did very well with two peas on a No 8 hook.

But later in the season, I couldn't get a touch on peas, and thought I'd try a worm to see if any perch were about. I got five chub between 2 and 4lb and every one of them spat out peas when I got it on the bank.

Then there was the February day I fished about a hundred yards upstream of Fred Taylor on the upper Ouse. Fred fished for roach with maggots on fine float tackle. I legered for chub with a lobworm on a No 6 attached to 1x. I caught a 2-pounder – and it had a bellyful of Fred's maggots, yet he never touched a chub all day.

Last month, Joe Taylor was legering in the Thame. The weather was cold and the fish were right off. Joe tried flake, crust and maggots, groundbaiting with maggots and bread, and for four hours never had a bite.

Then he tried a medium-sized red worm and had a chub of 2lb on his second cast with it. He brought it along to show me. Its mouth was full of bread, maggots and worms.

In the ordinary way, if you load a swim with maggots or mashed-up bread, you get chub on to it and they won't look at other baits. I've watched worms washed through a swim where chub were fed with maggots, and they wouldn't look at the worms, or at cheese, or anything but maggots. But that is when the weather is reasonably warm.

When it is cold, it may be that chub, which like all other fish eat less in cold water, eat only a little of any one thing. If they really are omnivorous, in every sense they may need a lot of different things in their diet.

Change of bait

In warm water, they can eat a lot of one food and change to another late in the day. In cold water, far less of any one thing might be enough.

(pages 144-5) *The shelter of the overhanging trees on the far bank provides a perfect haunt for specimen chub*

143

This may be true, or it may be all wrong. But in case it is true, I intend to try a change of bait, in a place where I know chub ought to be.

Of course, the logical comment is, 'Why groundbait?' There are times and places where I don't think it pays to do so in cold weather. An angler who knows his river really well and is positive about the whereabouts of the chub, can limit himself to flicking in a very few samples of his hook bait.

But in many cases such positive location is impossible; and judicious feeding on the 'little and often' principle can attract chub up from a long way down-stream. If on the way, they've eaten quite a lot of the ground-bait, it is quite possible that they may want something quite different on the hook – if the water is on the chilly side.

Of course, I may be barking up the wrong tree. It may be that changing the bait affects the way in which it is being fished, and makes it more attractive to the chub. Perhaps Bazley's chub wanted stuff like small bits of cheese – or maggots – whirling about in the current, and refused solid lumps of cheese paste.

Perhaps my chub at Offord wanted peas that rolled along the bottom and not ones that were tethered to a bit of lead, but were willing to grab at a worm that stayed in the current a bit. You can speculate as much as you like about why fish behave as they do; sometimes you hit on the right answer, and sometimes, more often, you don't.

It is worth remembering, though, that in warm water you usually do best with chub if groundbait and hook bait are alike. In cold water, you may get a chub on a hook bait that is quite different from the groundbait.

Causes of failure

Whether this applies to other fish, I cannot say. I've known some queer things happen, like big bream taking paste balls the size of tangerines when they wouldn't touch pieces the size of hazel nuts. I've known pike refuse a livebait and take a lobworm, and I've even caught a pike that had refused a fish and a worm on a lump of cheese.

There's no doubt that a change of bait will sometimes give you a fish you wouldn't otherwise have caught, but it is equally certain that much commoner causes of failure to catch fish than having the wrong bait are fishing the wrong place, choosing the wrong time, scaring fish or using the wrong technique.

13 December 1957

The chub

Although chub can be caught at almost any time during the coarse fishing season, I'm sure the best time to catch a really big one is from the middle of January to the season's end.

Chub fishing in summer is interesting and exciting, and specimen fish can be caught. But there is the need to use finer tackle because of the clearer water and slow current, and there is a quantity of rush and weed into which a hooked fish can bolt.

Bankside cover
Add to this the reluctance chub often show to take a bait from the bottom and you'll see that the chance of landing a big chub in winter is much better than in summer, provided one important thing is remembered about winter fishing.

Quietness and concealment are more important in winter than in summer.

Very few anglers believe me when I say this. But in winter, not only is there less bankside cover to screen the angler; the fish are lying much deeper in the water. A fish lying deep is better able to to tell when an angler appears on the bank – even when the water is coloured.

Coloured water
When you can't see the fish, you can't tell when you've scared them. But because you can't see them, it doesn't mean they can't see you.

In coloured water, they probably can't see you very clearly but they don't need to. All they need know is that an object has appeared on the bank that wasn't there before.

A small change in the amount of light from the sky, from one direction, is enough to alarm fish, and especially chub, which are more easily scared than any other British freshwater species.

Of course, they can feel the vibrations of your tread on the bank equally as well in winter as in summer.

If you remember the necessity of keeping out of sight and treading lightly, you can take advantage of winter conditions and use stronger tackle, fished at longer range.

Legering is much more effective in winter than in summer because then chub are much more keen to pick baits off the bottom. But don't be completely bound to legering.

The reduction in weed and rush often allows a long trotdown to be made with float tackle in winter, in a swim that could not be fished that way in summer.

If you have no results with leger tackle, in a swim that can be trotted, then change to float fishing and let your tackle go downstream as far as the swim allows.

This is a specially useful thing to try if you have been groundbaiting steadily. You aren't always sure where your groundbait is settling, or whether fish are taking it as it goes downstream or waiting for it to settle and then picking it up from the bottom.

You may, by rolling a leger in a series of arcs, contact bottom-feeding chub that are eating your ground-bait, but that system may miss the fish that are taking groundbait going down the stream.

Heaviest float

Float tackle is best for these fish; and don't use a tiny little float with only one or two shot. Use something heavy enough to follow the run of the current accurately and to run down steadily. A chub will pull the heaviest float under without any bother at all.

This change to float fishing after a spell of legering is specially worth trying if there has been a rise in water level recently, or if the place you are fishing is inclined to be rather swirly and turbulent. The two things often go together, of course.

Swirly currents are apt to lift your groundbait and carry it downstream, so that it doesn't settle, and this encourages chub to feed off the bottom, intercepting what the river is carrying along.

I have often taken some nice chub on float tackle, in fact the last five-pounder I had in the 1958–9 season was caught when I sent a float 40 yards further down the river than I had fished with the leger.

Even if float fishing doesn't get results at first, don't assume your groundbait has been wasted. After giving a swim an exhaustive searching, first with the leger, then with float tackle, try, if no result is forthcoming, moving to the next swim downstream.

It is surprising sometimes how far even a heavy kind of groundbait can go before it settles. Even if some of it has lodged on the bottom, a lot of the lighter particles may be going a very long way downstream; and as the heavier lumps are broken up by the current, small bits will start travelling downstream too.

This doesn't always bring fish upstream. Sometimes it has the opposite effect. If a small shoal of chub meets a stream of groundbait coming down the current, the fish may turn downstream to pursue bits of food that they've missed intercepting.

Fallen branches

So try everywhere in the line of the current and on each side of it. You may even find your fish a hundred yards or more below the place into which you put your groundbait.

All this means that when you hook that specimen chub you're so keen to catch, it will probably be at the end of a long line. If there are beds of dead rushes or any fallen branches or underwater bushes about, your chub will do its best to get among them.

The ability to decide in a fraction of a second after striking your fish, that it is no mere 2-pounder but THE chub you want, is important. You don't want to jump up and go pounding downstream, scaring all the fish, if what you've hooked can easily be brought up to where you sit.

Tough fighter

But when you know the fish you've hooked is worth spoiling your chances of bites for the next hour or more, if only you can land it, then you can get moving, so as to shorten your line as quickly as possible.

Nothwithstanding what game fishers say about chub not fighting, a 5-pounder hooked from January onwards is a very fast, tough, powerful fish; quite different from what it would be in May just after spawning.

You can't afford to let it romp all over the river on a long line. So shorten up and get a good pressure on as soon as you can.

When you've landed your big fish, you'll probably find your swim needs resting for an hour. But have a couple of casts before deciding to move; I've known cases where a second big one has been caught right away, in spite of all the disturbance of landing the first.

It doesn't often happen, but it's worth having a couple more throws, just in case.

8 January 1960

Get down for roach in winter

Catching roach in late autumn and early winter poses several problems, and anglers who persist in using the same methods that succeeded earlier in the season will be disappointed with the results.

More water and colder water is coming down the river now, and this means the roach will move from their summer haunts into slower and usually deeper water. And because the water is colder, they will be much less inclined to move after baits that are passing them at some distance.

Just how you fish depends on the state of the water, but choosing exactly the right method can make all the difference between a nice catch and a blank day. It's all a question of making sure the bait is fished very close to the bottom, and then deciding how and when to move it.

If the water is reasonably warm, anything above 45°F, the roach are likely to be in a moderate current, and if you can work ordinary float tackle down the current, you will probably do quite well. You can use nearly as much groundbait as you would in summer, but rather stiffer to make sure it gets well down to the bottom.

But between water temperature of 40°F and 45°F, you'll probably find the roach have moved into much slower water, even into real slacks where the water is hardly moving at all.

Behind rushes

Or you may find a shoal has taken up residence behind what is left of a bed of rushes, which slows the sub-surface current and shelters the fish. Then you must put your bait exactly where the fish are, and either let the current move it very slowly indeed, or use a tackle that anchors it so that the only movement it gets is what you give it by moving the rod or taking a bit of line.

For this you must reduce drastically the amount of groundbait that you use, making absolutely sure it goes in exactly the right spot. That can often best be done by moulding a small ball of groundbait on your shots and casting it out.

Remember that when you're fishing a place where roach have gone for shelter from the current, and because they don't like to move about when the water is cold, you can't expect thumping bites, even on waters where in summer the roach are confident biters.

Delicate biters

Sheltering roach take a bait quite delicately, and stay where they are. If you're fishing an anchored bait, you'll have a job to know when you've got a bite unless you use very sensitive tackle.

I'm sure it pays, when fishing in such conditions to have at least half your shots within an inch of the hook. Then the least movement of a biting fish is registered by the float.

Luckily, cold-water roach aren't so likely to spit the bait out quickly (probably because they move so slowly and therefore feel less drag from your tackle), so you don't have to strike very quickly. The main thing is to use a technique that will tell you that striking is needed.

Having the shots close to the hook lets you use crust cubes, which stay above the mud that is often found at the bottom of these slacker places where roach go in cold weather.

Crust is very good bait in cold water, for that and other reasons, not only for roach but also for dace and chub. I've known cases where crust has beaten maggots by ten fish to one, at this time of year.

Apart from anything else, a roach can suck the inside out of maggots, after which he'll eject the empty skins and you recover your tackle to find you had a bite you didn't know about.

151

But the roach can't do that with crust; if they want to eat it, they've got to eat the lot; though they will often get the crust off the hook without moving the float much, it is true!

I'm sure, though, that many more bites are received, and registered, on crust than on maggots when roach are lethargic and sheltering in slack water.

Use 'landmarks'

Finding the right place to fish, and the exact spot in that place, often takes time and the problem is one that needs a persevering approach. It may take a couple of hours of carefully searching a likely place inch by inch, before your tackle arrives in the spot where the fish are; so it is very important to keep constant check, by looking at 'landmarks' on exactly where your float is.

When you eventually do get a bite, you want to get your tackle back in the same place, and it is surprising, sometimes, how hard it is to remember exactly where that was, after you've played, netted and unhooked your fish, in which process you must have taken your eyes from the water.

I try, directly the first bite comes, to pinpoint exactly where the float was, and I don't mind too much if I miss that first fish, as long as I know where I got the bite.

In this fishing, there's no such thing as 'near enough'. You must try to be *exact*, and if you succeed you will often have a netful of fine roach on days when less careful anglers are saying 'Oh, they were right off today!'

8 December 1961

Just how big will perch grow?

Izaak Walton's statement about the size of perch, quoted in Ken Seaman's article in *Angling Times* of 22 June, is interesting to consider.

How big do perch grow?

Walton's 'almost two foot long' seems to me quite possible.

Such a perch would weigh between 9 and 10lb and I don't think that is entirely beyond reason.

Of course, there would have to be quite exceptional feeding available to produce such a fish, but this applies to any species.

It isn't so long ago that Dr. Regan laid down that the limit of growth of carp in Britain was about 25lb. Events have since shown that this was an underestimate and that there are many waters in this country where carp can reach 30 to 35lb.

Few over 5lb

Only in the most exceptional waters do they grow bigger; but where they are introduced into such a water, they grow to quite fantastic sizes. Redmire pool holds, without doubt, one or two fish in the 60 to 70lb region.

In good average waters, perch reach a weight of between 4 and 5lb. The number of perch over 5lb recorded and authenticated beyond all doubt, is very small indeed. Any angler who catches a 4lb perch has done as well as he can reasonably hope for.

But it seems to me that if in an exceptional water carp can grow to about twice the size they reach in average waters, perch may do it also, and that there may be places where perch between 8 and 10lb are swimming about.

In the early 1950s, Arlesey Lake in Bedfordshire used to yield large numbers of big perch. The biggest taken weighed only 3oz under 5lb but those anglers who caught big perch regularly from Arlesey lake at that time all know that bigger perch existed there than any that were caught.

I once saw a perch on an angler's line seized by another and bigger perch before it could be brought to net. The bigger one eventually let go and the smaller one was landed. It weighed no less than 3lb 2oz!

The one that grabbed it could never have swallowed it; big perch often have exaggerated notions about what they can get down their throats.

But I don't think that fish can have weighed less than 6lb and it could easily have weighed 7lb or more.

My experiences with the perch at Arlesey have been misleading, I think. None of us who caught those big perch there ever had them on any bait but worms, though we tried live and dead fish of various sorts and sizes, as well as spinners of all kinds. The artificial baits never did any good, and the real fish caught only eels and small pike.

Since then, not only Ken Seaman and Alan Pearson, but several other anglers, have found that in other waters a dead fish or a piece of dead fish, lying on the bottom, is an excellent bait for big perch.

I have myself seen several perch between 1lb and 2½lb taken on dead baits that had been put out for pike or eels.

Intelligent fish

The trouble about livebaiting or deadbaiting for perch is that unless you know exactly where the perch are, your bait is much more likely to be taken by an eel or a pike. You're likely to be broken time and again if you use tackle suitable for perch, or else there's such a disturbance in landing the pike or the eel that the perch are scared off.

Despite the fact that perch are occasionally caught on pike tackle or eel tackle, I am sure that using strong lines and wire traces greatly reduces the chances of tempting big perch, who are intelligent fish and very sensitive indeed to tackle-drag or stiffness. They'll spit out a bait instantly if they feel anything suspicious.

Don't be misled by the behaviour of small perch, which are often so determined to swallow a bait that they'll drag along a big float or a heavy leger lead, and even try to pull your rod in.

Big perch behave very differently and one of the secrets of success in the days when we caught those big ones at Arlesey was to arrange the tackle so as to cause the least possible check to a biting fish.

The Taylor brothers and I have found that exactly the same applies to the big perch in the upper Ouse. The least check, and the bait is rejected.

Perch will undoubtedly take large live or dead baits, and the use of these in experimental fishing might easily lead to records being broken.

It is worth remembering though that really big perch will take small baits at times, sometimes in preference to big baits. I've known the Ouse three-pounders reject with contempt minnows, gudgeon and large lobworms, yet bite keenly on brandlings or cockspur worms.

The first step
Only last year, I fished a well-known perch swim with both small and large worms and also with minnows and never had a touch. Changing the tackle with the intention of trying for a few roach, I baited a No 16 hook with a single maggot and had a perch of 2¾lb at the first cast.

Rather than commit myself to a policy of using any particular bait, I prefer to concentrate on the problem of locating the big perch.

If that problem can be solved, it isn't difficult to offer different baits in turn until one is found that the perch in that place and at that time, find acceptable.

27 July 1962

Roach tactics for fast waters

When the river is running high and the water is cold, most of the fish will be in slow or slack water. But high, warm water often brings fish into the fastest water.

When they are feeding eagerly, they can be caught there by longtrotting, legering, or, if the fast water is reasonably close to the bank, by stret-pegging, with the angler downstream.

There are times, however, when the fish bite very shyly. With most species, this simply means greater concentration and faster striking by the angler, who has to watch out for delicate bite indications.

With roach, however, it often happens that none of these methods will succeed, because these fish can eject a bait like lightning if they feel too much drag or check.

Long-trotting
With any form of downstream fishing in fast water, they are likely to feel a check all too easily when they take the bait. The tackle is in

a straight line, or nearly so, from hook to rod-tip in downstream legering and stret-pegging, and in long-trotting, a fairly heavy leading, with a big float is needed to fish the fast water. Its inertia is high, and shy roach easily feel it.

The roach that takes the bait doesn't have to move to feel the drag of a long-trotting float tackle. The current carrying the tackle applies a pull as soon as the fish stops the bait. Too often a roach will eject that bait before the angler can strike.

If the nature of the swim allows it to be used, there is a method that overcomes these troubles. It is upstream float-fishing, or upstream stret-pegging, if you like to call it that.

Its success depends on correct choice of float and lead, and it is often necessary to do a good deal of experimenting with floats of different sizes, and different loadings for these floats, before you get it right.

The idea is to arrive at a combination of these that can be cast upstream, where, instead of coming back down the current, the tackle will just hold bottom with the top of the float showing above the surface.

Bites are shown by the float rising and moving downstream towards the angler. Since the whole tackle is only barely resisting the current-pull before the bite comes, the least touch will cause it to shift.

Obviously, such a method cannot be used in a swim full of whirls, boils, eddies and cross-currents. The floats would be lying flat one second and out of sight the next, before the bait was even touched. The method is mainly one for smooth glides where the depth is not too great.

Just how deep a swim can be and still respond to this method depends on too many factors to list here, but this can be said: You can try it on any swim that looks possible, and see for yourself.

No special kind of float is needed; I use ordinary quill ones like porcupines, turkey quills and swan quills.

Of course, the float must be set a lot farther from the lead than the depth of the water. How much further depends on the current and the weight of the tackle, but twice the depth is about right to start. You can make adjustments after you've seen how the float rides.

Current rhythm

With practice, you can tolerate a certain amount of swing and dip of the float in the current. In fact it doesn't really matter if the float disappears now and then, provided you've learnt the rhythm of the current.

It is, of course, possible for a bite to occur that takes the float under; a fish that moves upstream after taking the bait will cause it.

The indication is usually easy to distinguish from the dip caused by current movement, partly because it will almost always be out of the rhythm of the current and partly because the float will not only dip but move positively in an upstream direction.

There's no need to worry about it, in any case, because most of the bites will be the kind that makes the float rise and move downstream.

If you are using the method in a fairly deep swim and casting well up, there may be some slack immediately following the bite, so a sweeping strike will be needed to take this up and tighten on the fish.

Opinions differ

Among anglers I know who use this method, opinions differ about how far the lead should be from the hook. When baiting with crust cubes, I think it should be quite close, no more than an inch or so.

For other baits, much depends on current speed and depth. For fast shallow swims, I like to keep the distance between hook and lead very short, regardless of what bait I'm using, but for slower, deeper water this distance can be extended to a couple of feet or more.

I like to have my shots on a doubled-over link of nylon, with a single shot used as a stopper. It is much easier with this to alter the position relative to the hook or to add or subtract shot, and if a fish does decide to move upstream after taking, it will feel less drag because it only has to move the float and one shot. With roach, that is usually too much anyway, but not always.

This upstream float-fishing doesn't have to be static. You can cast your tackle upstream and leave it where it settles, or you can inch it back bit by bit, so as to cover more water.

It's an advantage to have a fairly long rod, because as I said earlier, there can be considerable drop-back on the bite, especially in a deepish swim, and also because if you're inching the tackle back, the bite may catch you with the rod in a position that makes striking less easy.

A long rod allows you to take up more line for any given hand movement.

In your favour
This upstream fishing has another advantage – the instant you hit your fish, he's coming in your direction and the current is in your favour.

Groundbaiting needs watching. If you throw it from where you sit, it will probably not go as far upstream as it should. I find it best to walk up, with as little disturbance as possible and without showing myself on the skyline, and put groundbait in from where I'd choose to fish if I were tackling the swim from upstream instead of from below.

Don't be afraid to use a large float, and a lot of shot, if the current and depth demand them. All the fish that move downstream after biting aren't going to feel more than it takes to dislodge the tackle, and that can be as little with four swan shot in a fast swim, as it is with a single BB in a slow one.

This isn't a dead-easy method of fishing, and it needs some practice to get the best out of it. It's worth a little perseverence, though, because there are times and places when it will get you fish that would be difficult if not impossible to catch by more conventional styles.

28 January 1966

Keep it simple to catch fish

With the usual crop of reports of big tench captures, in both numbers and size of individual fish, coming in at this time of year, I have had the expected pile of letters from young, and from older but inexperienced, anglers asking for advice about how to catch them.

I think the best advice I can offer is that the simple, straightforward, well-tried methods are the ones to try, and to persevere with until you're absolutely certain that they won't work.

Don't think for a moment that in saying this, I am in any way critical of the special methods that have been developed by highly experienced specialist tench fishers and specimen hunters. I do think, however, that young anglers and comparative novices are often misled by reading articles advocating special methods.

Your tench fisher of long experience tends to assume that everyone knows as much about the normal, simple ways of fishing as he does and will find no interest in articles describing them. It is only when he comes across a special case, where these methods fail, and when he evolves a new way that succeeds in that special case, that he thinks he has got something worth writing about.

Many new ideas
Well, so he has, and what he writes will prove most interesting and useful to others of similar experience. Unfortunately, those with considerably less are likely to think that his new, special method is the one they should promptly employ for all their tench fishing.

I suppose something similar might be said of methods used in other kinds of fishing, except that there seems to have been rather more in the way of new ideas for catching tench, lately.

Let me therefore say that it is not at all common to find tench that can't be caught on the simplest kind of float or leger tackle. Use a monofil line of strength suitable for the size of fish you hope to catch and the conditions in which they live. Six pounds bs is a good all-round size. Put a simple float on the line, like a goose quill or a porcupine, of a size that will show about ¼ inch above the surface when loaded with a single swan shot.

Tie on a size 6 eyed or spade-end hook, pinch on the swan shot about a foot from the hook and set the tackle so that instead of showing ¼ inch of tip, you see about three-eights when you've cast out. This shows your shot is on the bottom.

Now bait with a big fat lobworm, or a pinch of flake, or about ten ordinary maggots, and you're in business. Your chances are better if you've dragged the swim beforehand and treated it to a helping of groundbait. If there's a breeze, or drift, that keeps blowing the line round dragging your tackle out of position, remove the top float cap, or slide it down next to the one at the bottom, and sink your line above the float.

If waves are high enough to make seeing the float difficult, take it off, and use a dough-bobbin or its equivalent.

If one swan shot won't give you enough casting range, double a bit of nylon over your line above the shot and pinch more shot on its two ends, close enough to your line so that the loop in the extra bit of nylon can't slip over the fixed shot.

Basic tench methods

There you have the simple techniques of fishing for tench that, in most waters, will do all you need. These methods, or ones similar in principle, account for 99 per cent of the tench caught every year, small, medium, large and extra large. And when they fail, the commonest reasons are that the tench aren't there, or if they're there, they're not feeding. Or if they're there and feeding, the angler isn't fishing correctly. It is quite rare to find that any other reasons exist.

Sometimes, in heavily fished waters, tench get a bit choosy and by using the lift method you can catch them when the ordinary style won't. There's nothing very complex about that. You move your swan shot closer to the hook – within an inch – and you attach your float bottom end only.

Float will rise

It's called the lift method because the bite is usually, but not always, indicated by the float rising and, if you delay the strike long enough, it may even lie flat.

But you should strike directly it begins to rise. The bait is crust and you use a fairly small piece as a rule, not because you can't fish a big bait on lift tackle but because where tench are willing to take big baits there's no need for fishing lift style. A useful size is about as big as a small pea when wet, on a size eight or perhaps a size 10 hook.

Sometimes even this doesn't work and you can then try a single maggot on a strong 14 hook, or a grain of stewed wheat on a size 12, treating the tench to a few handfuls of maggots or wheat every now and then. Notice, we're still talking about simple well known methods and common, easily prepared baits.

You may find a tench lake or pool where none of these methods work. If there is thick, deep bottom mud or silkweed, try using crust and increasing the distance between shot and bait till you think your crust is just above the top of the mud or weed. If the bottom is, on the other hand, firm, and there are swan mussels about, try baiting and groundbaiting with pieces of these. I've known them succeed where other baits didn't, but not very often. No need for special tackle or methods. Use the same as you'd use for lobworms.

Feeding habits similar

We all know that there are quite a number of waters inhabited by tench, where some of the fish are bigger than any ever caught. There has been speculation about whether these monster tench, anything between 10 and 15lb, have developed feeding habits that are different from those of smaller but still quite large tench. I've wondered about that myself in the past; but I've now come to think that the diet remains the same.

There are several simple reasons why these monster tench aren't caught. They swim in ones and twos, but behave as separate shoals, not mixing with bigger shoals of similar tench. They are not present in large numbers anywhere.

Groundbaiting attracts many smaller fish that get the bait before the bigger ones, if the latter come into the same area. And if one of these whoppers is hooked, it breaks the tackle. They have tremendous power, these outsize tench. They're not like other fish where the pulling power gained by a big one is offset by a loss of speed. Tench aren't very fast at any size, so their increased size is all gain.

When extra big tench are caught, it's usually the ordinary, well known methods and baits that catch them, and I would advise youngsters and novices to stick to those methods and baits until they've acquired much more experience.

18 July 1968

Once hooked twice shy – that's the roach

For reasons that are still not very clear, there has been a very considerable decline in the numbers of roach and dace in some waters. Disease, pollution and predation by zanders have all been blamed; perhaps one day we shall discover what the truth of the matter is.

On some waters, however, poor catches of roach are not inevitable. Plenty of good healthy roach are still there, though they are not often caught. There are reasons for this.

In the first place, if there are fewer roach they will be harder to locate. In the second, with more food available for each fish, they will be fussier about what they will eat. Thirdly, even before roach began to get scarce a high proportion of the fish, and particularly the larger fish, had become educated.

I know there are people who claim that fish have no intelligence and are utterly stupid. Don't you believe it. A fish that has been caught once will be harder to catch again, specially on the bait that caught it the first time. I know that now and then a case occurs where a fish is caught twice or even three times in the same day and on the same bait. These cases are rare exceptions. More commonly, a fish that is caught and returned won't take another bait for weeks.

Bits of metal

Now, on many heavily-fished waters, roach have been caught several times in their lives. They've also seen other roach caught, and they've learned a thing or two about how to avoid capture. There must be millions of roach in Britain now that know it's unsafe to eat maggots, specially maggots tethered to filaments and containing bits of metal.

But there are still gaps in the knowledge of these fish. They may know all about maggots, or casters, or hemp, depending on what the anglers who fish the waters where they live have been teaching them. They still don't know about all the possible roach baits. A crafty old fish that won't look at a maggot may still take confidently a grain of stewed wheat or a neat cube of breadcrust.

If you want to catch them, then try some bait that has rarely or never been used on the waters you fish. Never mind what others tell you. Bait reputations always outlast the real value of the baits. Often a new bait scores heavily when it is first used; I've just explained why. Within a short time, anglers come to feel that without that bait they might as well not go fishing at all. They go on using it long after its value has worn off. Because, don't doubt it, wear off its value certainly will, and the more fish it catches the faster its value will fall.

Just one among many

That is one reason why I don't care for bait bans. We hear people say 'This must be barred – if its use continues there won't be a fish left!' The truth is that by allowing its use to continue, you make sure that its effectiveness will decrease. Whatever it may be, with use and in time it will become just one among many useful but not specially deadly baits or flies.

Of course, in dealing with highly educated fish, you have not only the bait to consider but also its presentation. Many a cunning old roach that would simply shift aside to let a trotted bait go by, will sidle along and pick up a bait that is lying on the bottom. Or he may refuse a bait on the bottom, refuse one suspended below a float, but take one that is slowly sinking. I used to catch some specially crafty roach by letting the bait rest lightly on top of silkweed, with the shots on a separate link.

Others I have come across wouldn't tolerate having to lift even one BB shot, so I devised an extra long antenna float, set so that a roach could lift the bait several inches before it felt the weight of the lead.

There were some roach in a part of the Kennet and Avon canal where the light was the deciding factor. They positively refused every bait we offered them, no matter how presented, until after dark. Then they took big bits of flake so positively that if allowed they'd have nearly pulled our rods in.

One day, on a part of the Hampshire Avon, I fished a swim for barbel that needed a ¾oz Arlesey bomb to hold against the strong current. I was baiting with cubes of cheese the size of lumps of sugar. Nobody knew that roach were there; nobody else was catching roach on that stretch, not even anglers who were fishing hard for them. I got twenty or more up to 1¾lb on my cheese, size 6 hook and a 6lb line.

One more example

Who would dream of fishing for roach with such tackle and such big baits? Nevertheless, that is what caught them, and it is one more example of fish being taken by a different bait and method from what is commonly used and accepted by anglers – but not always accepted by the fish!

One more example. I used to fish for carp in a small, very clear lake in Hertfordshire, which also held roach. You could easily catch fifty roach there in a day, with fine line, float tackle, a small hook and the usual roach baits like maggots, paste or crust. Most of the fish were about 3-4oz and you never got one as big as ¾lb.

Not by roach-fishing methods and baits, that is.

The carp in that lake liked lobworms. We therefore fished huge worms on size 4 hooks and 9lb lines – no lead – and we caught carp. We also caught roach, really big ones. The biggest I caught weighed 2lb 13oz and I had lots between that weight and about 1½lb. We never got these big roach on roach tackle and baits, only on the big worms fished on heavy tackle but, be it noted, leadless and floatless tackle.

Alternative baits

Let me say that I am by no means advocating the use of heavy tackle for roach fishing, nor am I saying that using very big baits is often the answer. What I am trying to point out is that there are plenty of roach about that have learned to avoid conventional roach tackle, rigs and baits, but which can be caught by experimenting with alternative baits and way of presenting those baits.

Not only that, but sometimes you may catch bigger roach, a lot bigger, than you would have taken by the usual methods, if you try something quite different.

This sort of thinking doesn't only apply to roach, of course. All kinds of fish can learn from experience and that means that changes of method, of bait and even of fishing times and places may be needed to catch them.

You can catch them

So don't be in too much hurry to say that all the roach in your water have been killed by disease. In many cases, some of them have been. In some cases a great number may have perished. But there are few waters where none is left. You can catch them but you will probably have to try different ways from those that used to be successful. Controlled impatience is what you need, the impatience that leads you to try different things instead of sticking to the same old routine and blaming lack of fish for your failure.

28 August 1969

Seek big roach when shadows lengthen

In spite of the effects of disease on the numbers of roach in many of our waters, there is still some good roach fishing to be found up and down the country.

If roach are in a water at all, it's a poor angler who can't catch small ones. A very skilful angler can catch large numbers of small ones, but it takes more than skill to catch a few big ones.

A big roach is a crafty chap. He's fussy about what baits he will take, when he will feed, where he will feed and the behaviour of what he feeds on. He is easily scared and he's lazy. Above all, he doesn't like bright light.

In all the fishing I've done for big roach, and it's plenty, I've never done much good in summer when the sun has been high enough to penetrate the water. When the sun is high in the sky, a great deal of its light penetrates the water, but as it gets lower, more and more is reflected from the surface. When the sun makes an angle with the surface of about ten degrees or less, hardly any light penetrates.

Of course, some light is reflected from the atmosphere and from any clouds that may be in the sky, but penetration by direct rays from the sun practically ceases at this angle of ten degrees, and when it does, the big roach begin to feed in earnest.

I might add that this sun angle is important with all kinds of fish.

Critical angle
Of course, it sometimes happens that a big roach gets itself caught under a high-bright sun, but the angler whose ambition is to catch big roach consistently knows that his best chance, by far, of suc-

165

cess is from the time the angle of the sun falls below 10°, until about an hour after sunset.

On some waters, roach also feed well from about an hour before sunrise, until the sun has risen above the 10° angle, but in my experience the evening feeding spell is far more consistent and reliable than the morning one.

The next most important thing to remember about big roach is that a bait anchored to the bottom usually catches far more fish than one that is moving with the stream, or hanging below a float, or both. Methods like laying-on, float legering, stret-pegging, and plain legering, are much more effective for specimen roach than straightforward float-fishing, despite the fact that they involve extra problems about dealing with bites.

The third thing I want to stress is that, generally speaking, maggots aren't good baits for big roach. I've caught upwards of a hundred roach over 2lb on maggots, so you may wonder why I say that. Well, almost all of the big roach I've caught on maggots were taken from places where there weren't any small roach, and even

The dream of every angler – a 2lb roach. Big roach are crafty but often come on the feed as dusk falls (Ron Wright)

in those places, the very biggest roach were caught on flake or breadcrust.

In most waters, where there are roach of all sizes, maggots catch more roach than bread baits, and they may even catch some fair sized ones too. But I still say that if you're after the biggest roach, you'll do better with bread baits than maggots.

What about other baits, like stewed wheat and hemp? Well, if you stick to fishing your bait hard on the bottom after the sun has got below ten degrees, you'll usually do best with bread, even in waters that hold minnows, bleak, gudgeon and other nuisance fish. Now and then the nuisance fish are so numerous and so ravenous that you may be forced to use stewed wheat or hemp, but I would only do so as a last resort.

Now, what about dealing with bites? Big roach are very sensitive to resistance from the tackle when they take a bait. That's why so many bites are missed when leger tackle is used, specially at short range. The biting roach feels the resistance of the rod top, or the swing tip, and although there may be a good positive bite registration, by the time the angler strikes, the roach has blown the bait out of his mouth.

Really big river roach don't feed much in fast water. They're lazy. When they start feeding in earnest, it is nearly always in a slack near to, but not in, the faster water. That's where the current deposits natural food, and your groundbait.

There's a lot of talk about getting groundbait down so that it stays down in fast water. If you want to catch big roach, fish where the current has taken your ordinary groundbait. Don't struggle to make special groundbait stay in fast swims that big roach don't inhabit or anchor your tackle with heavy leads in such swims either.

Rig up a float tackle that carries one swan-shot. Set the distance between float and shot at about 18 inches more than the depth at the edge of the fast water. Cast out and let the current take the tackle down and round until it anchors itself with the float top showing.

Anchors float

If the current pushes the float under, draw the tackle into slacker water till the float stays up. Don't put on more shot and a bigger float.

167

In slower rivers, you can use a smaller float and lighter shotting. But in the faster rivers, I'd say that any current that's too fast for laying on with one swan shot and a suitable float is too fast for the biggest of the roach – the ones you want to catch.

So the question of tackle resistance really resolves itself, doesn't it? The only snag is that after dark, you can't see a float, unless you shine a light on it and that can present difficulties and objections.

So take the float off, but not before you've put a marker on the line so that you can put your bait without the float, exactly where it was with it. Then use a swanshot on a sliding loop of nylon, with a nylon stop to keep it at the right distance from the hook. Detect bites with a bobbin-type indicator, preferably a permanently luminous one.

If you're going to fish on after dark, you may as well fix your swan shot up with a sliding loop, and attach the nylon stop, right at the start, using a float attached by two rubber caps, which lets you remove it easily.

25 June 1970

Perch – how to catch big 'uns

Disease has struck the perch population of many waters in recent years, but some are left where big perch may still be caught, and I have no doubt that those afflicted will eventually recover. So let's talk about how to catch big perch. First, river perch.

Look for swims alongside rushes, with hard sand or gravel bottoms. Use a float attached by means of a shaped valve rubber at each end, so that it will go either way through rushes without catching. A length of peacock quill is as good as anything. Either build a swan shot or its equivalent in lead wire or foil into the bottom of the float, so as to make it self-cocking, or pinch a shot on the line touching the bottom of the float when it is set at the correct depth.

The float must be buoyed enough to carry extra weight near the hook. That will depend on current speed, but in most good perch swims, a couple of BBs a foot from the hook is about right.

Line strength – not less than 4lb. Hook – size 6 for big worms, size 10 for small red worms.

Cast so that your float, which travels ahead of the baited hook through the air, hits the rushes and falls close to them. The baited hook will swing down underneath so that it, too, is close to the rushes. Now let the current take the tackle downstream, keeping it as close to the rushes as possible.

Give each likely swim fifteen to twenty minutes trial, trying first big lobworms, then changing to small red worms. Change the hook when you change the bait.

A day that is misty, or a fine drizzle, in September, October and November, is best for this.

Now for lakes. Ten years ago I'd have said, wait until mid-September, then leger with a big worm in the deepest place you can find, up to 40 or 50 feet. Experience on trout reservoirs has partly changed that. Legering in the deep holes in autumn and winter is still a good method and the best time of day is between 10am and 3pm; the sunnier the better.

But you can also catch big perch on tandem lures, fished either on fly-fishing tackle, or with a fixed spool reel, monofil line and a suitable lead three feet above the lure. You don't need swivels because tandem lures don't spin.

A fine catch of autumn perch, taken on worm bait from Arlesey Lake

For the fly fishing use a Hi D (ultra fast sinking) line, which sinks at a rate of 1 foot every 3 seconds. Start by fishing at 15 feet; if no results, try deeper. In summer and early autumn I've caught lots of big fish with fly tackle at 20 to 25 feet.

Most two hook tandem lures will catch perch but my most successful pattern is the Hanningfield lure, tied on two No 8 long-shank hooks. White df wool bodies ribbed with silver thread, a hot orange cock hackle wound at the rear and clipped; hot orange throat hackle with a wisp of blue hackle at the front of the orange; under wing of white goat hair with speckled turkey feather fibre above it.

I've caught hundreds of perch over 2lb with it, and other anglers tell me they found it highly successful too.

Livebaits are highly rated for perch by some anglers, but not by me. True, many big perch have been taken on minnows, gudgeon and small roach or rudd, but I think it likely that worms or tandem lures would have been equally successful, while the great drawback to livebaits is that they're liable to attract pike. Unfortunately, the tandem lure catches pike at times, but not nearly as often as small livebaits.

All the perch I've caught over 3lb were taken on worms or tandem lures, except one, and that took a jointed floating pike plug.

Big perch will sometimes pick up a small deadbait that has been cast out and allowed to lie on the bottom, but fishing that way means catching eels most of the time.

The time when a small deadbait can be used with success is when you see perch chasing fry, which they often do for a quarter of an hour or so early in the morning in summer and autumn, when the mist is lifting and before the sun gets on the water.

You can see the perch dashing about, making the fry leap in all directions, and sometimes a big prickly dorsal fin breaks the surface. Cast a small dead fish, on a single hook, where all this is going on, and start drawing it back very slowly as soon as it hits the water. Or use a tandem lure on a fly rod, with a floating line.

Sometimes similar activity occurs at odd times when you're fishing for roach, dace or bream and using a groundbait that breaks up small as soon as it hits the water. A few seconds after throwing in a ball of groundbait a shower of fry erupts into the air, to escape

170

the perch, or sometimes the chub, that is attacking them.

Put a tiny deadbait in the middle of the next ball of groundbait, attached to your hook, lob it out and wait for results. You may catch a chub, you may catch or be broken by a pike But there's a good chance you may catch a big perch, or perhaps more than one.

Now let's be clear about one thing. Perch aren't spread around in any water, like raisins in a Spotted Dick pudding. In rivers, in summer, the big ones are in ones and twos, but they shoal up in the autumn. In lakes they're in shoals all the time. Shoals don't stay long in one place.

They move about, and you've got to find them or you won't catch them. Don't imagine that because you've caught a few in one spot yesterday, that you can be sure of catching some more from the same place today. You may, or you may not. So be prepared to search for them. If you put your bait or lure where they are, you don't usually need to wait long before you catch one. Twenty minutes is usually long enough to wait.

On a big water, if you can't find the perch, it may be worth trying a big pike spoon. You won't very often catch a perch on it, but they'll follow it, and if you have a big worm out on another outfit, you can sometimes lead the perch to that by spinning the spoon past it, making successive casts with the spoon at various different angles.

You can also search a wide area by using a big float and a floating line, and casting across the wind, so that the tackle is dragged round in a wide arc, with the bait either lightly dragging bottom or just off it. The bait can be a big worm, or a small dead fish. At Hornsea Mere, they used to use the complete set of gill rakers from a small perch as bait, with the wind drift technique, but I think a big worm or small fish would do just as well.

A good big perch is the most impressive fish that swims, to a real angler, so it's worth going to a lot of trouble to catch one.

11 September 1974

60lb carp did exist

I am often asked what I think about the chances of a new record being achieved for carp. It's a most difficult question to answer because so many factors are involved.

For a new record to be established, the first essential is the existence of a fish big enough. The old saying 'There are bigger fish in the sea than ever came out of it' is not always true. When Albert Buckley set a new carp record in 1930, with a fish of 26lb, I think it likely that at that time there were very few carp in England much bigger. A rumour went round not long after Buckley caught his record fish that a 30-pounder had been found dead at Mapperley, and this may well have been true, but I doubt very much if any carp as heavy as 40lb existed at that time.

It was about then that Major Don Leney began importing a fast growing strain of carp from Germany, the Galician strain. There are varieties of carp, just as there are varieties of cattle. Galician carp grow bigger than some other strains just as Friesian cattle grow bigger than Jerseys or Guernseys. By importing this strain of carp, the foundation was laid for bigger carp to appear in the future; but growth rates in fish differ from those in mammals.

If there isn't enough grub for mammals, they become thin and emaciated, and perhaps die of starvation; but fish with too little food stay quite healthy; they just don't grow as big as they would have if they'd had more food.

Suitable food
Consequently, a carp with a high growth capability will only grow big if it lives in a water where there is plenty of suitable food. Very few waters have enough fish-food to enable Galician carp to achieve their full growth capability. In fact, it is possible that no water in Britain is good enough for them to do so. Here we have to consider not only food but climate. For several months of the year, carp are eating less food because water temperature is too low, even if the food is available.

Even in an established strain of carp, all fish aren't alike. The growth capability varies greatly between one fish and another.

One of those early Redmire carp, admired by Dick Walker and its captor, Pat Russell. This 27lb mirror was taken in August, 1956

Fred Taylor and I put eighty little carp, all of the same size, into a stretch of canal; three years later we recovered seventy-three of them, whose size varied between 3lb and 14lb. Only three or four of them had reached between 13 and 14lb, so you can see that perhaps one in twenty has the capability to grow to record size.

These wide differences in growth rate are found in artificially bred strains. Carp in the wild state have much more uniform growth rates, because natural selection tends to standardise the type found in each water. Natural selection almost never operates in favour of the greatest size. We can easily see what sort of carp is produced in Britain by natural selection, because there are plenty of them about. They're called wild common carp, or 'wildies'; fully scaled, much longer and slimmer for a given weight than recently imported varieties, and seldom reaching weights of more than 14 or 15lb.

When that great icthyologist, Tate Regan, wrote in the late 1920s that the upper limit for carp in Britain was about 25lb, he was talking about what we call 'wildies' and I think he was about right.

The point is that natural selection will eventually reduce the growth potential of imported strains of carp to about that figure, unless new importations are constantly made. My information is that the Galician strain that Major Leney used to import is no longer available, even if Ministry of Agriculture regulations allowed it to be imported.

We are therefore faced with a situation in which the chances of catching 40lb carp are likely to decline steadily, and almost certainly this decline has already been taking place for several years.

It is a long time since I fished Redmire Pool from which my 44-pounder was taken, but from what people who still fish it tell me, fewer real monsters are seen than there used to be.

Old age

Back in the 1950s, I would guess that there were perhaps a half-dozen carp in Redmire bigger than my record fish, the largest being perhaps as heavy as 60lb. All these big fish have almost certainly died of old age by now, and I doubt whether fish bred since will have grown quite so large. It would appear that there are many more carp there now to share the food supply, so they cannot grow quite so fat.

To sum up, there are perhaps three or four waters that could hold carp of 45lb or so, but fish of that size are not numerous anywhere; perhaps three or four in each of those waters I would guess – and it is only a guess – that as the years pass the numbers of such fish, already small, will decrease, and the time may well come when there isn't a carp in Britain over 30lb.

In the meantime, what kind of angler is most likely to set a new record before it is too late? Well, there are hundreds who have the angling ability. The only difference between catching 20lb carp and catching 40lb carp is that there are plenty of 20-pounders but very few 40-pounders. It doesn't take any more skill or knowledge to catch 40-pounders than it does to catch 20-pounders; it's just that there aren't many 40-pounders to which the skill and knowledge can be applied.

However, it does take quite a lot of skill and knowledge, combined with perseverence, keenness and suitable tackle, to catch

Dick and the rest of the Redmire anglers in the fifties certainly believed in comfort. Fred J. Taylor serenades the author as they relax in their ex-army bell tent between fishing sessions (Pat Russell)

big carp at all. Very few are taken accidentally. The carp record has been broken five times since the beginning of 1916, and every time by an angler who was fishing for carp.

There's no way of fishing for carp that lets you pick out 40-pounders from among the much more numerous smaller fish; so a would-be record-breaker must expect to do a lot of carp fishing, unless he enjoys a fantastic stroke of luck, a factor that can never be eliminated from fishing of any kind.

If I were asked to depict the kind of angler most likely to break the carp record, I'd point to someone like Kevin Clifford; young enough, at 28, to put up with many hours of fishing, often in uncomfortable conditions; thoroughly well informed in all aspects of carp fishing, from reading and experience combined; able to spend time after carp; able to afford the best available tackle; blessed with a methodical as well as an inventive mind, and most essential of all, able to fish where one or two fish heavier than the present record exist.

I hope whoever does set a new carp record will be someone who understands how important records are. The real carp angler, in my book is he who consistently catches carp. How big they are is largely irrelevant.

16 July 1975

The 50lb pike

When Martin Gay points out the folly of setting your sights too high, I am fully in agreement.

When a young man still in his twenties says to me, 'I've had two seasons of carp fishing, but I've only caught thirty double figure fish and nothing over 18lb, what am I doing wrong?' I'm apt to tell him that he'd better give up fishing because if he persists in it he's going to spend the rest of his life in a constant state of disappointment.

A similar attitude has now spread to pike fishing. Anglers of limited experience, and often with limited opportunity, seem to think that they ought to catch 20-pounders every day, and that it shouldn't be very long before they catch a 30-pounder.

This is all ridiculous. Most anglers can consider they've had a nice day's sport if they catch three or four pike between 5 and 8lb. As for carp, anyone who catches a few double figure fish in a season has done well.

Climatic
Where I differ from Martin Gay is in his assessment of possibilities. In the first place, it is a mistake to assume that fifteen years or so is the life span of pike everywhere. Pike vary considerably between one water and another. Irish pike have been isolated from English pike, for example, for hundreds of thousands of years, and will certainly have evolved somewhat differently – not enough to have become a different species, but enough to differ in some respects. There is reason to think that Irish pike have a better growth rate but a shorter life span.

Next there is no evidence whatever to indicate that extreme climatic conditions have any effect on pike growth. The German

176

record is quite a lot higher than ours, yet winter in Germany is much more severe, and you can drive a lorry over the ice that forms on the Russian lake from which a 90lb pike was caught.

If in fact, protracted spells of cold water did inhibit pike growth, then we should expect pike to do better in a Scottish loch, with depths of hundreds of feet than in Fen drains, or the Broads, where the water is shallow and can be chilled to near freezing point right to the bottom. In deep lakes, the water below 40 feet or so never drops below about 42°F, and the pike can always find water warm enough to feed in.

Culling

Then there is the question of fertile water. Highly fertile water is not necessary to provide ample food for pike, if there are runs of migratory fish such as salmon and sea-trout. Many Scottish lochs have such runs, but in most of them there is a rather limited supply of non-migratory species. Among the exceptions is Loch Lomond, the southern half of which is very fertile indeed. It grows roach to at least 2lb, perch to 3lb; it has a huge population of good sized eels; flounders migrate from the sea, as do runs of salmon and sea-trout, and on top of all this, Lomond has huge shoals of powan, on which the pike feed extensively. There is good reason to think that many of these fish, certainly the powan and the perch, move into deep water in winter, where the pike follow them.

As for culling and over-fishing I am at a loss to understand how Martin Gay related this to pike growth. It is usually thought that the fewer fish there are, the bigger they grow. Provided an individual pike isn't caught, one would suppose that the more other pike were removed, the better the survivor would fare.

However, all this is academic as far as Loch Lomond is concerned, for its area must well exceed 100 square miles; that's equivalent to about fifty Grafhams. Several thousand anglers would have to be fishing Lomond every day to have any significant effect on the pike population. They don't, because they can't. Most of the pike in the loch live out their lives without ever seeing an angler's bait or lure. I doubt if many readers have any conception of the sheer size of Lomond. It's as long as the English Channel is wide. If you poured all the water from Grafham into it, you'd hardly notice any rise in the level.

Now I come to what can be deduced from the size of pike skulls. It is quite wrong to say that they do little but cloud the issue. We know the measurements of several skulls from big pike whose weight is also known. A skull 12 inches long has to belong to a very big pike, from whatever water the fish comes.

But if we have caught large numbers of pike from a particular water, and have found that they all have heads that are much smaller in relation to their body size than average, then we say that a 12-inch skull must have come, not just from a very big pike, but from a monster.

It happens that Loch Lomond pike do have very small heads in relation to body size, compared to pike from the Broads or the Fens. Much the same applies to pike from some Irish waters.

Authentic

Now I don't want to give the impression that anyone can spend a few days on Lomond, or on other likely Scottish lochs, and come home with a 40-pounder in the boot of the car. Many good anglers have fished on Lomond and failed to catch a pike half that size. But that doesn't alter the fact that 40-pounders are most certainly there. Not only that; I, personally, am certain that there are pike well over 50lb in Lomond and other lochs too.

It seems to me that it is quite ridiculous of Martin Gay to say 'I cannot see Scotland producing an authentic 40 pound pike' when Scotland has already produced more than one such fish, the best known being Tom Morgan's fish of 47lb 11oz. There is absolutely no doubt about the size of that fish.

Nor have I any doubt that the fish I saw at the end of Fred Buller's line, in the same spot where Morgan's fish was caught, was even bigger. After fifty years of catching big fish of all sorts, I am not a bad judge of their size, and when I am in error, it is invariably an underestimate.

I do agree that a very likely place for a pike to reach 40 pounds or more is a large trout reservoir, where in addition to coarse fishing there is an annual stocking with tens of thousands of trout. These

A skull 12 inches long has to belong to a very big pike, from whatever water the fish comes. This skull, held by Ken Taylor, was 12⅝ inches long and came from a pike estimated to weigh more than 70lb

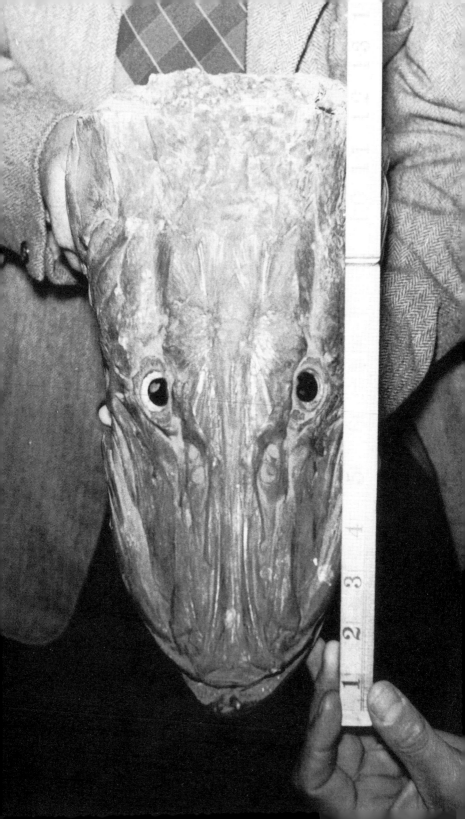

correspond to the natural stocking of lochs like Lomond with sea trout and salmon. In both cases there is a large influx of pike food that does not depend on the resources of the loch of reservoir. I think it is likely that Grafham already holds pike of 40lb.

14 December 1977

Scrap of a lifetime

The barbel has always been a favourite species with me. It grows to large size and its fighting qualities are second to none. It may not be able to reach quite the speed of a carp, nor will it produce spectacular leaps like a trout, but weight for weight, and with regard to the strength of the tackle, I know of no other fish that goes on fighting for so long or with such sheer power.

Until the late 1940s, my experience of barbel was limited to catching one or two small ones by accident in the River Lea. They spelled it Lea in those days! But in 1951 I caught a few barbel from the Great Ouse, including one of 9lb, and was greatly impressed by them. I should add that I got those on cheese paste while fishing for chub, so I cannot claim much credit for these captures.

In 1953 I visited the Royalty Fishery for the first time, on the Hampshire Avon, in the final leg of the match I fished against the late and greatly respected Tom Sails, of Lincoln.

On that day I caught two barbel, 7½lb and 10¾lb, fishing a swinging leger with a ¼oz Arlesey bomb on a 6lb line, with a No 6 hook baited with cheese paste. Those two fish, with a couple of ½lb chub, gave me the match, plus the keen desire to catch more barbel; and from then on I fished the Royalty many times over several seasons.

In those days, all you needed was a few pounds of ground bait, consisting of chopped cheese mixed with well-balanced bread and bran, and either cheese paste or cheese cubes on the hook. I caught a lot of barbel, including some double figure fish.

Maggots

One evening I had three, 9lb 12lb and 12½lb. I stopped fishing

A typical Kennet barbel, thick and powerful. While the author's largest from the water was a mere 7lb, he did once lose a fish estimated at 15lb!

eventually, being barred by the management for having criticised the way in which the place was run, but I would probably have stopped going there anyway after maggot mania set in.

The fishing became a competition to see who could afford to throw in more maggots; the fish became preoccupied with maggots, and the result was that no more barbel were caught than in the bread and cheese days; it just cost a great deal more to catch them.

The place also became grossly overcrowded, often with people using wildly unsuitable tackle such as sea rods and 4oz grip leads; no limitations placed on the numbers of tickets sold, and it was common to find people fishing only a few yards apart.

I remember once having a barbel of 11lb on, and before three minutes had passed, two other anglers (?) moved to within a touching distance, one on each side, and cast heavy leads into my swim!

After I'd explained what I proposed to do if their actions lost me the fish, they moved off and reported me for threatening be-haviour, with no little justification for the charge, but nothing came of it.

So I stopped fishing – or was stopped from fishing – the Royalty, and sought barbel on the middle Avon and also on the Kennet. The Kennet is a lovely river and I caught a lot of barbel from it, but never a big one. I did hook one or two big ones, one of them a real monster which I think must have weighed 15 or 16lb, but the tackle I was using was quite inadequate and I lost these big fish, though I had great sport with the smaller ones. The best barbel I ever had out of the Kennet weighed 7lb.

Monsters

On the Avon, I fished mostly at Ibsley, through the kindness of Colonel Crow, and also on Lord Manners water at Avon Tyrell. In both places the barbel were far from numerous and proved ex-tremely difficult to catch.

With Fred J. Taylor and Pete Thomas, we went down weekend after weekend without catching any barbel, though we had a lot of fun with roach, dace, chub and trout.

Just occasionally, a barbel did get caught. I had a couple of 11lb at Avon Tyrell, and some smaller ones, plus a 10½-pounder, at Ibsley. The frustrating thing was that we could often actually see the barbel and some of them were monsters, far bigger than the record which then stood at 14lb 6oz, and in my opinion still should. We tried every bait we could think of and these great barbel ignored them all.

During this period, we had evidence of the presence of record fish in the Avon, because Charles Cassey caught one of 16lb by accident while salmon fishing and Lady Rothes, also spinning for salmon, caught a barbel of 17½lb at Bisterne.

Fred Taylor, Pete Thomas, Colonel Crow and I agreed that many of the fish we saw were a good deal bigger than that; I remain certain that we saw 20-pounders.

The best barbel I ever caught came from the Somerley water at Ibsley. Pete, Colonel Crow and I had been out on a reconnaisance and spotted a big barbel, lying all by itself on a small patch of gravel, only a little way out from the bank. That evening I returned to the spot; the barbel had gone.

I had a split cane carp rod, a fixed spool reel holding 11lb nylon, a 1oz lead and a No 1 hook, which I baited with three very large worms. I lowered these on the patch of gravel where I'd seen the barbel, and then walked about 20 yards upstream, paying out line as I went.

There I sat until after dark, resisting the temptation to try for some big chub that were active near the far bank. I didn't even have a shot at a mink I saw with my catapult; it was one of those warm, quiet evenings when you want to blend with the landscape rather than engage in much activity.

Suddenly there was a tremendous bang on the rod top and I had to grab the rod like lightning to stop it from going into the river. The fish, whatever it was, was going down stream very fast, making the slipping clutch fairly sizzle, and I wondered whether I'd hooked a salmon.

Tired

A bankside tree limited the distance I could follow the fish, so I gave it a lot of stick and it swung across the river right to the other side, where there was very little current.

There it tugged and plunged about for some time, but I had strong tackle and was eventually able to move the fish back till it was under the rod. Then it shot off upstream and dug itself into some thick streamer weed.

Every time I pulled it out it shot back in; it did that several times. In the end, it tired, but I had a hard job to net it because of the current pressure on the big carp landing net I was using.

This really needed two hands, but I had a rod in one hand and a torch in the other, so I had to jam the torch between my knees and do the best I could with one hand on the net. It was a real pantomime, but I succeeded at last.

The fish weighed fractionally over 12¾lb, still the biggest I've ever caught. I slipped it back and after a time spent holding it right way up, it dashed off. I'll never know whether it was the same fish that I'd seen earlier in the day, or whether there were more in the same area because I packed up after catching that one.

12 April 1978

Ten degrees below

For those who can fish waters holding barbel, this species is one of the most exciting, and without doubt the most puzzling, of all the coarse fish.

It is often possible to make big catches of barbel of modest size, specially from rivers where there are large numbers, but putting a big one, upwards of 10lb, on the bank, is a very different matter.

Early in the coarse fishing season is a good time to try because up to about the middle of July, barbel seem more willing to eat a variety of different foods, including small fish like minnows, small gudgeon and roach.

Why dead fish lose their appeal later, nobody seems to know, but there's no doubt about their effectiveness in June and early July, the only drawback is that small dead fish are also eaten by other species, including perch, pike, chub and above all, eels.

You need no pre-baiting or free offerings if you try small dead-baits for barbel, nor is special tackle necessary. Just fix up an ordinary leger outfit, with a single hook passed through both lips of the bait. If you feel a tap and wind in to find only the head of the bait left, and the body missing, neatly cut off, blame a chub, not a barbel.

Golden

If you want a big barbel, try to fish a river clear enough to let you see the fish, or at least the golden side of a fish as it turns on the gravel. Even that gives you a good idea of size. Not every likely looking barbel swim holds barbel at all and even fewer hold the big chaps, so it is a great help if you can actually see the fish.

Failing that, try to find out from other anglers which swims have produced big barbel in the past; except where exceptional floods have altered the river bed or banks, big barbel tend to inhabit the same spots year after year.

Unfortunately they don't stay in these swims twenty-four hours of every day. They often move out at dusk and go foraging in another part of the river, often several hundred yards from their daytime haunts. You can't predict where they'll go, and they seldom go to the same spot on successive evenings.

So all you can do is put something they like to eat into their day-time swims, just when they're feeling hungry and thinking about moving away to feed. If you get it right, this will hold them and give you a chance of catching one or two.

Critical
I think the time to do this is when the angle of the sun to the water has gone down to about 10°. That's a critical angle for all fishing because below 10°, the direct light from the sun is completely reflected and the underwater scene goes through a tremendous change in illumination. Many species of fish start feeding in earnest at this time.

Wherever possible, I like to use big baits, like lobworms, small dead fish, cheese cubes, ¾ inch across, similar sized bits of paste, with or without meat or trout pellet additions, pieces of lamprey, and so on because big baits let you use big hooks and strong lines.

Barbel are among the most powerful of freshwater fish, and in weedy waters, fine tackle is not sensible. If, however, you have to use small baits like maggots, casters, hemp or corn, you don't need to go for very tiny hooks; all these baits can go on a size 10, and it matters not if a lot of the hook shows.

Nor, in my experience, are very fine lines needed; I've never had to go finer than 5lb or 6lb. If I'd fished finer, I might have hooked more barbel, but I am sure that many of the big ones I've caught would have been lost.

On the Avon, I've caught quite a few big barbel with anything from one to four small hooks, attached to fine nylon, in their mouths, all put there by anglers fishing too fine for fish of that size.

When are small baits necessary? The answer, simply, is when the barbel won't take big ones. This often happens on heavily fished waters where large quantities of small baits, mostly maggots and casters, but hemp on some waters, are being constantly thrown in by anglers, but there are times when only small baits work, even without that.

I think it's a question of encouraging the barbel to feed when they otherwise wouldn't by presenting them with food consisting of large numbers of very small pieces – what anglers now call 'particle' baits.

Because barbel swims are, fortunately, often found close

alongside the bank from which you're fishing, such baits can be put in with a bait dropper, and I'd always rather use one than a swim-feeder where possible. I don't like bulky objects hanging on my line when I'm into a big fish, specially in weedy waters.

But where you have to cast more than a few yards, the swim-feeder is the best choice when the bait is maggots or small red worms. The latter being a more useful barbel bait than most anglers seem to think.

Barbel can be caught on float tackle at times, but I nearly always leger, using either the smallest Arlesey bomb that barely holds bottom, or a string of swan shot. Unless you touch leger, you will fail to detect many of the bites. I've had days when I've caught as many as eight or nine when if I'd used any other method of bite detection, I wouldn't have had a single fish.

Barbel at times produce these buzz-bites, like a vibration up the line, or like wind in telephone wires. I don't really know how to describe it but you will know if you feel it. So hold the rod, rested on your thigh, in one hand, and the line between butt ring and reel in the fingers of the other.

23 July 1980

The 'Buckden Breamer'

Every coarse fish angler knows that certain species of fish, such as carp, tench and bream, send up characteristic bubbles when feeding at the bottom, but it is not generally known that these were of commercial importance in the 18th and 19th centuries, before the advent of the modern synthetic type.

Bubbles were in great demand in the heyday of railway expansion, which was in turn responsible for the boom in the spirit-level industry in the early years of the last century; and my great uncle 'Ezer was for many years Head Globulist to Messrs Buckden Bros., whose spirit-level factory stood on the banks of the Great Ouse at Offord.

Those were the days of real craftsmen; and at Buckdens' they made spirit-levels that were second to none. Men like George

Stephenson, Will Jessop and Isambard Brunel went to Buckdens; and Buckdens, under the technical supervision of Ebenezer Mycock – my great uncle 'Ezer-gave them the acme in spirit-level design and workmanship – the brass-bound 'Buckden Breamer.'

The secret of this marvellous spirit-level was jealously guarded, and when at the age of 87 great uncle 'Ezer was accidentally killed by a whippletree falling on his head from the hayloft of a barn, it was widely believed that the secret died with him.

I can now reveal, however, what that secret was. It lay not, as Buckdens' competitors mistakenly supposed, in the quality of the spirit, but in that of the bubble.

In 40 years of research and study, great uncle 'Ezer had discovered the secret of obtaining a deliberate, slow-moving bubble, He got his bubbles from bream. Every morning, just at sunrise, a big, flat-bottomed punt emerged stealthily from a water-gate at the side of the Buckden factory. Along each side of the punt, on hands and knees, each with a bundle of glass tubes and a funnel, were girls, recruited locally, ready to catch the precious bubbles.

The punt was propelled and steered by an ancient waterman with life-long experience of the river, who, because of the damp, always had a rum issue; and it is interesting to note that this practice gave rise to what in later years was to become a common expression among drinkers. Having filled his rum-pannikin, the old fellow would pause to scan the surface of the river; then, on spotting the bubbles, he would first cry 'Bottoms up!' and then drain the pannikin, his cry being simply an admonition to his crew to get on with their job.

In later years, when the old chap had to retire, the firm ran into some difficulties with his much younger successor, difficulties which were solved only by the acquisition of a set of blinkers from Newmarket, but not before the punt had been accidentally capsized more than once.

While bream-bubbles were the mainstay of the Buckden Brothers' business, great uncle 'Ezer knew that these were not the ultimate in bubbles. Tench bubbles were even better when they could be obtained in a sufficiently large size. Unfortunately, tench bubbles are nearly all very small indeed, and the occasional one that was big enough was so rare that collection was not economically possible, and even the few that were collected varied in size,

so that tubes had to be specially made to fit them. Being an enthusiast, however, great uncle 'Ezer spent much of his spare time in search of king-size tench bubbles, and during his lifetime he collected seven, one of which was incoporated in the Company's silver-mounted ebony master level. Four more went into specially-made levels that were supplied to the Royal familes of Europe and one, I understand, is still kept at the Royal Observatory at Greenwich. The level containing the remaining one is a priceless family heirloom; and from my own experience I can vouch for the fact that to use such a level is a wonderful experience.

Now, alas, Buckdens' is no more. It was neither competition nor the industrial revolution that killed the firm, but disagreement between the brothers who were its joint proprietors. The elder, D'Arcy, was level-headed for the most part, and acting on their late father's dying wish, he and the more spirited younger brother, Cluny, had agreed to confine their social activities, in the form of drinking bouts, wenching, etc, to opposite sides of the river. Even to this day the village of Offord, which straddles the river Ouse, has its opposite halves known locally as Offord D'Arcy and Offord Cluny, and it was a shortened form of the surname that gave rise to the term 'Regency bucks.'

Unfortunately, on the day the firm received the Royal Warrant (having supplied a 'Buckden Breamer' to the resident carpenter at Buckingham Palace) Cluny went on a mad spree which culminated in his pursuing, by swimming, a red-headed wench across the river. This, D'Arcy not unreasonably resented. The ensuing fracas led to an estrangement and Cluny withdrew his capital from the firm, using it to set up a rival establishment that incorporated a carp-pond, from which he expected to extract superior bubbles of all sizes.

Unfortunately – and probably because by now the seasoned advice of great uncle 'Ezer was not available to him – he found the idea would not work. So profuse were the carp bubbles that his employees could seldom avoid catching more that one in their funnels, and as everyone knows, a spirit level with two or three bubbles in it is useless, specially if they are of different sizes.

Fred J. Taylor unhooks a 2lb rudd, taken from a Lincolnshire lake during a fishing session with the author

Demented by his failure and impending bankruptcy, Cluny chose a dark night to set fire to his brother's factory, and our family records contain a vivid account of the fire; it records that the popping of over-heated spirit-levels could be heard for miles around.

In those days, insurance was unknown, and so the firm of Buckden Brothers perished; but although its existence has been long forgotten, it is interesting to note that the village railway station, though now closed by Beeching, still bears, not the simple name 'Offord' but 'Offord and Buckden,' thus fittingly commemorating the old firm – and its bubbles – to which the railway pioneers owed so much.